THE EVERYDAY RICE COOKER

The

EVERYDAY
RICE COOKER

Soups, Sides, Grains, Mains, and More

DIANE PHILLIPS
PHOTOGRAPHS BY *Jennifer Causey*

CHRONICLE BOOKS
SAN FRANCISCO

To Susan and Jerry Webman for going the distance

Library of Congress Cataloging-in-Publication Data available.

ISBN 978-1-4521-2781-1

Manufactured in China

Designed by Stitch Design Co.

Food styling by Marian Cooper Cairns

10 9 8 7 6 5 4 3 2 1

Chronicle Books LLC
680 Second Street
San Francisco, California 94107
www.chroniclebooks.com

INTRODUCTION

The electric rice cooker, sitting on the counter in countless homes and restaurants across Asia and around the world, makes cooking rice as easy as flipping a switch. I lived in Japan for three years when my children were young, and the first purchase I made upon our arrival was a rice cooker. I was curious about what it could do; and I was up for trying any appliance that I could set and forget. All the instructions were in Japanese; but with a bit of help from my housekeeper, I set out to make rice. Then I graduated to rice pudding, soup, stir-fries, and even some stews. This was a terrific little gizmo, and I cried when I had to leave it behind with my Japanese friends because the electric current in Japan is different from that in the United States. When I returned to Southern California, I found a similar rice cooker at a Japanese market and grabbed it.

Always the curious cook, I now find myself using the rice cooker to make one-pot meals, with rice cooking on the bottom and fish or another protein steaming in a basket above. I have even prepared smoked salmon in the rice cooker. Just set it and forget it, or set a timer. It's that simple, and the rice cooker really does all the work. And it's energy-efficient, too.

Developed in postwar Japan by Sony and Mitsubishi, the first rice cookers looked like wooden washtubs with electric coils in the bottom. The problem with these rice cookers was that they had to be watched, since they had no timers or shut-off mechanisms. In the mid-1950s, Toshiba developed the grandfather of the rice cookers we know today: one with a timer. Its popularity was enormous, and the factory could not keep up with demand. Further development brought the on/off rice cooker—a machine that detected the absorption of the liquid in the rice cooker and turned off automatically. More recent developments include fuzzy-logic rice cookers, which can be programmed for different types of rice. And there is now a rice cooker that can be programmed from your smart phone! These days, you can find rice cookers in every price range and size, including pressure-induction rice cookers.

A rice cooker cooks with steam. The process is simple, the results are delicious and healthful, and cleanup is minimal. It's true that steamed chicken can be bland and unappetizing and that steamed vegetables often wimp out, but there are tactics for producing flavorful foods in a rice cooker. Marinating proteins like fish and poultry gives them deep flavor, which comes through in the finished dish. And browning them before steaming creates rich color, taste, and aroma. Balance the protein with a complementary grain cooked in a flavorful liquid in the very same pot, and you'll have a delicious, flavor-packed meal in 30 to 40 minutes. Toss vegetables with some good olive oil, a few herbs or spices, or just salt and pepper and add them to your rice-cooker steamer basket during the final minutes of cooking a pot of grains for perfectly crisp-tender vegetables. The prep for most of these dishes is minimal: readying one bowl, a bit of chopping, and arranging the food in the rice cooker.

When you're making a one-pot meal in a rice cooker, you can choose from a number of methods: One is the steamer approach, where there is rice or another grain in the bottom of the pot and protein (chicken, meat, or seafood) or vegetables steaming on top. When cooking this way, it's all about fine-tuning the timing so that the protein or veg is perfectly done, not overcooked, when the grain on the bottom is ready. For example, for fish fillets cooked in the steamer basket over rice, you would put the fillets in about halfway through the cooking time, rather than cook them for the full 30 to 40 minutes that it takes to cook the rice. With poultry, meats, and vegetables, the same often holds true. Follow the timing directions given in the recipes, and your dishes should be perfect every time.

Another approach is to sauté and then simmer, as when making a soup or stew. For dishes like these, you will have to time the cooking, since the liquid in the pan will not evaporate and the machine will not shut off automatically.

Finally, there are the rice- and grain-based dishes that steam in the pot, like pilafs and risotto. For each type of recipe, I will guide you through the process to turn your ingredients into a delicious rice-cooker dish.

Which foods are best to cook in a rice cooker? I find that the best proteins are chicken and seafood, since they cook quickly and are tender when steamed. Boneless chicken breasts and thighs are especially terrific, as bone-in portions tend to take too long to cook and will throw off your timing. Meats (beef, pork, and lamb) tend to toughen up when steamed, although ground meats in preparations like meatballs, sausage, and stuffed cabbage leaves turn out well. Tender vegetables and leafy greens should be stirred in once the dish is done and allowed to steam for 5 minutes with the rice cooker covered but on the keep-warm setting or turned off. Root vegetables can be steamed in the rice cooker and should be cut into evenly sized chunks to cook at the same rate.

The culinary inspirations for rice-cooker meals are large and varied, including the Mediterranean, Asia, and Central America. Each one-pot meal will entice you and your family with its flavors. All you need to do is get the ingredients and set the machine, and your dinner will be ready, quick as a wink. And you'll have only a few dishes to wash.

But what I love most about a rice cooker is its versatility. It allows me to quickly and easily make a one-pot meal, such as paella or curry, but keep the kitchen cool and the stove top clear. If I were to cook the same dish on the stove, I would probably use at least two different pans and would need to attend to the cooking; with a rice cooker, the machine does the babysitting and then turns itself off at the end of the cooking time. What's more, a rice cooker's countertop footprint is smaller than that of a slow cooker, but it can still provide a satisfying dinner for a small family. Since just my husband and I live in our home, a rice cooker is the appliance of choice when I want to make a one-pot meal for the two of us. With a rice cooker on your countertop, you, too, will find yourself preparing easy, wholesome meals that include healthful grains, legumes, and lean proteins for you and your family.

ALL ABOUT RICE COOKERS

——

In this section, I'll try to demystify how rice cookers work, what to consider when purchasing a rice cooker, and how to use the rice cooker to prepare the recipes in this book.

HOW RICE COOKERS WORK

After you add rice and water to a rice cooker, the machine brings the water to a boil quickly and then lowers its temperature. Water boils at 212°F/100°C. Once the water has been absorbed and the rice is cooked, the temperature of the rice begins to rise above 212°F/100°C. The machine's thermal sensing device notices this rise in temperature, and the machine automatically turns off or switches to the keep-warm setting. This is why when cooking foods with a lot of moisture, such as soups and stews, you need to time the cooking. Otherwise, the rice cooker will continue to run until all the moisture is gone.

With the fuzzy-logic machines, you will have to reset the machine to the regular cycle after sautéing, turn the machine off, and then start again on the regular cycle.

WHAT TYPE OF RICE COOKER SHOULD I BUY?

A rice cooker is a relatively simple machine, with just a housing unit, a removable bowl for cooking, a cover, and a power cord. You can find basic models in any housewares store, Asian grocery, or department store. More expensive machines are sold in kitchenware stores. Cleanup for any of these machines is simple. I would recommend following the instruction manual for your specific product, but a soak in hot soapy water and a good scrub with a nonabrasive sponge is really all you need to clean up the rice-cooker bowl.

ON/OFF RICE COOKERS: These are the simplest, least expensive type of machine. They are nothing more than a basic steamer, with only an on/off switch. The machine will turn off automatically when the rice is done, and the ambient heat in the machine will keep the rice warm for about 30 minutes. If you have an on/off rice cooker, I will remind you to allow the rice to steam for 5 to 10 minutes after it is done (with the machine turned off). Other rice cookers are automatically programmed to continue steaming after cooking.

ON/OFF/WARM RICE COOKERS: This type of machine costs a bit more because of its more complex design. It will switch itself over to "keep warm" (like a slow cooker) when the rice is done. Be aware that sometimes the keep-warm setting can be pretty hot, and rice can stick to the bottom and burn if left in for more than a few hours.

FUZZY-LOGIC RICE COOKERS: These sophisticated rice cookers can cost at least twice as much as a basic on/off machine. "Fuzzy logic" refers to the artificial intelligence programmed into its computer chip, which allows the rice cooker to think for itself. (It is also called a "micom" rice cooker, from the word *microcomputer*.) The machine will make minute temperature adjustments in response to the volume of rice and water, just as you would if you were cooking a pot of rice on the stove top. Fuzzy-logic cookers can be programmed to cook white, brown, or sweet (sticky) rice; grains; porridge; and legumes. They also have programmable functions, so you can come home from work to perfectly cooked rice that is ready and warm.

Some manufacturers are now producing fuzzy-logic pressure rice cookers that are faster, more efficient, and more precise than standard fuzzy-logic cookers. These machines work on the principle that food cooks more quickly under pressure, just as it does in a pressure cooker on the stove top. The very latest innovation in fuzzy-logic machines uses induction heating along with pressure. In induction heating, the heat is generated by an electromagnet. Instead of coming from a single source in the bottom of the rice cooker, the heat fully surrounds the rice cooker's inner pot, for more even and consistent cooking. These two types of super-advanced machines make ultra-fine-tuned adjustments based on what's in the pot, and they produce perfectly cooked rice every time. But keep in mind that they cost as much as six times the price of basic on/off rice cookers.

Is a fuzzy-logic rice cooker worth the cost? In my experience, after using each type of rice cooker for the recipes in this book, I can say that the old expression "you get what you pay for" applies to rice cookers. Although inexpensive rice cookers can do the job, if you plan to use the appliance often, especially for one-pot meals, and if you rely on the keep-warm setting, a fuzzy-logic machine can't be beat. Your budget will determine which machine you buy. The lower end of the fuzzy-logic machines produced perfect rice during testing, so I would only spend the money on a higher-end fuzzy-logic machine if you plan to use it more than two or three times per week. The keep-warm setting on the basic model won't burn the food in the bottom of the pan, and it will maintain a perfect temperature for up to 12 hours.

RICE COOKER SIZES AND ACCESSORIES

Rice cookers come in several sizes. Small 3-cup/720-ml machines cook only enough rice for a family of three or four (without many leftovers). They are too tiny to cook one-pot meals, even on a small scale. Then there are midsize 5- to 6-cup/1.2- to 1.4-L rice cookers, which are the perfect size for a family of four or five. This is the cooker size that I used when developing the recipes for this book; I refer to it as a medium rice cooker. The next size up is a 10-cup/2.4-L rice cooker, which can cook enough rice to feed an army. Note that the size of the cooker refers to the quantity of cooked rice it produces. A 6-cup/1.4-L cooker will yield 6 cups/1.2 kg of cooked rice.

Within the past few years, some manufacturers have come out with machines ranging from 4 qt/ 3.8 L to 6 qt/5.7 L that are not only rice cookers, but slow cookers as well. And some of these multi-cookers are also pressure cookers, which can cook meals in half the time. These multifunction machines perform well and may appeal to cooks who do not have pressure cookers or slow cookers. But the size of the rice cooker you buy should be determined by how many people you are cooking for and how often you think you will use it.

A rice cooker comes with a measuring cup that has a capacity of approximately ¾ cup/180 ml. If you use the recipes in the instruction booklet that comes with your rice cooker, you will need to use that measuring cup. But for all the recipes in this book, I have used standard measuring cups to measure liquids as well as rice and other grains, and have given metric equivalents.

Most rice cookers also come with a steamer tray, plate, or basket. If yours didn't or you've forgotten where you stashed it, I highly recommend buying a silicone steamer, available in most housewares stores. Nonstick and dishwasher safe, it's a terrific tool for any kitchen, whether you use it in a rice cooker or in a stove-top cooking vessel. Silicone steamers are my favorite type of steamer.

If you plan to steam food in layers—say a protein and vegetables—without grains in the rice-cooker pan, you might want to purchase small stackable bamboo steamers that fit into your rice cooker. Make sure they will fit in your cooker with the lid closed.

A kitchen timer is also essential. You will need it for the one-pot meals in this book that require you to keep track of the time and turn off the cooker manually.

When you take your rice cooker out of the box, sit down and read the instruction booklet carefully; every machine is a bit different, and you should become familiar with the brand that you buy.

ABOUT THE RECIPES IN THIS BOOK

As noted previously, all the recipes in this book have been tested in 5- to 6-cup/1.2- to 1.4-L rice cookers, both basic on/off models and fuzzy-logic machines. But for simplicity's sake, the recipe instructions call for a "medium" rice cooker. For those of you with fuzzy-logic machines, if the recipe requires special fuzzy-logic settings or functions, I have included instructions for those as well. A small 3-cup/720-ml or large 10-cup/2.4-L machine is not recommended for this cookbook.

As with any kind of kitchen appliance or cookware, after a few uses, you will get to know your rice cooker and will be able to make adjustments to perfect the dish. Whichever size, type, and brand of rice cooker you choose, it's a good idea to start by making a simple pot of rice and then go to the next level and try a one-pot meal.

PANTRY STAPLES

Here is a list of a few items to keep on hand for making delicious meals in your rice cooker.

BIRYANI PASTE: If you like Indian food, this is a great addition to all types of dishes, not just biryani. The paste is sold in jars and can be found in the Asian food section of well-stocked supermarkets. Or it can be ordered online. The ingredients in biryani paste vary, but it is generally flavored with coriander, cumin, onion, ginger, dry mustard, turmeric, chili powder, and garlic. Some versions include cinnamon as well. Patak's is a good brand.

BLACK PEPPER: The difference between freshly ground and preground black pepper is like night and day. Using a pepper mill to grind peppercorns as you cook ensures that the pepper you add is aromatic and flavorful. Much of the black pepper that is sold preground has already lost its essential oils.

BROTH: Find a brand that you like and stick with it. There are so many brands on the market, many of which offer low-sodium or nonfat versions, that it's really a personal choice. For most of the recipes in this book, you will need chicken or vegetable broth, but you should feel free to choose a broth that will complement your main course, such as beef, seafood, or mushroom.

CANNED TOMATOES: For rice-cooker meals, I prefer canned chopped or crushed tomatoes. If you would rather use whole tomatoes, crush them in your hand before tossing them in the cooker. Fresh tomatoes in season can also be substituted, but for pantry dinners, canned tomatoes are a great thing to have on hand.

DRIED HERBS AND SPICES: These should be stored in airtight containers, where they will keep for up to 1 year. If you don't smell much when you unscrew the lid of a dried herb or spice, it's time to replace it. Thyme, bay leaves, whole oregano leaves, rosemary, red pepper flakes, and ground cumin are the ones I always have in my pantry. My favorite blend of spices and herbs is curry powder, which varies in degree of spiciness. For a medium-spicy curry powder, try a standard one. Hotter curry powders, such as Madras or vindaloo, can be substituted, but make sure your guests like to play with fire. Sautéing brings out the flavor and aroma of most types of dried herbs and spices, so whenever possible, add them to the pan and heat them briefly before pouring in any liquids.

EXTRA-VIRGIN OLIVE OIL: Buyer beware—in the supermarket, most bottles labeled simply "olive oil" are not extra-virgin olive oil. Extra-virgin is the first cold press and should say so on the label. Plain olive oil can be a mixture of different oils, in addition to olive oil. And some "light" olive oils are not lighter in calories, just lighter in flavor. I use first-cold-pressed extra-virgin olive oil to give a dish a flavor base, before adding other ingredients. It's the foundation of many Mediterranean dishes.

GARLIC: Fresh garlic adds flavor; preminced garlic has a processed flavor. Buy a head of garlic and use it!

GINGER: Fresh ginger adds an exotic note to many dishes. For grated ginger, simply peel with a vegetable peeler and grate with a rasp-style grater. Ginger will keep for up to 1 week in a cool, dark place. If you don't have plans to use the ginger in the near future, peel it and cut it into slices 1/4 in/ 6 mm thick. Place the slices in a clean jar; cover with sake, mirin (Japanese sweet rice wine), or dry sherry; and store in the refrigerator for up to 2 weeks. After 2 weeks, the acid in the wine will begin to "cook" the ginger, and it will become soft and spongy. You can keep the remaining rice wine refrigerated for up to 2 months; it will give a gingery flavor to stir-fries and salad dressings.

HOT SAUCE: A dash or two of a vinegar-based hot sauce, such as Tabasco or Frank's RedHot, brings out the flavor of some foods and really perks things up. When using other types of hot sauce, such as Sriracha or Cholula, add them carefully, drop by drop, because they may be too spicy for some people.

PARMIGIANO-REGGIANO CHEESE: Although it's not stored in the pantry, Parmigiano-Reggiano, the undisputed king of cheeses, is a staple in my refrigerator; I use it to flavor many dishes. Blocks of Parmigiano will keep, tightly wrapped in the refrigerator, for up to 2 months. Once grated or shredded, it will keep in an airtight container for up to 3 weeks. Sublimely flavorful, with a nutty aftertaste, Parmigiano is the only cheese to use on some pastas and in risotto. Save the rinds for tossing into soups, stews, and sauces; they soften up and add a delicious flavor to the pot.

SALT: Sea salt has a clean, pure flavor. Table salt often has a processed taste that can take away from the flavor of the dish. Many chefs use kosher salt, because the large crystals can be easily picked up and tossed into dishes, where they dissolve quickly. I prefer sea salt and have a salt grinder to grind the coarse grains. Use the type of salt that tastes good to you, whether it's kosher salt, preground fine sea salt, flaky salt like Maldon, or freshly ground sea salt.

VEGETABLE OIL: There are many vegetable oil options on grocery store shelves, but I like to use canola oil. It is usually made from genetically modified seeds, though, so look for a canola that is non-GMO. I also like grapeseed oil, which is more expensive. I use these oils when I need a neutral taste, one without the assertiveness of extra-virgin olive oil, so that it won't dominate the flavor of a dish.

A FEW TIPS FOR SUCCESS WITH YOUR RICE COOKER

• *If using milk or dairy products in the dish, coat the inside of the rice cooker with nonstick cooking spray or oil. This will help with cleanup.*

• *It isn't easy being green: Fresh green herbs can sometimes turn an unappetizing shade of khaki when steamed, so add them at the end of the cooking time.*

• *I always rinse rice in a sieve under plenty of cold running water. I have found that when using the rice cooker, if I don't wash the rice, the grains tend to stick to the bottom of the pot. I will remind you each time you need to wash the rice or any other grain in need of a good rinse.*

• *I find that cutting a protein into bite-size pieces before cooking yields more servings than if the protein were left whole. One chicken breast half may be enough for four, or even six, people when combined with a grain and vegetables. This means that your food budget goes farther when you make one-pot meals in a rice cooker.*

• *If you have no time to prep, a cruise down the salad bar at your local supermarket can yield all the precut vegetables you need to make a terrific vegetarian rice-cooker dish when you get home.*

BASIC RECIPES

———

ABOUT RICE

Almost half of the people in the world eat rice daily and depend on it as a staple food. Grown in flooded paddies, rice plants look like tall grass; they start out green and eventually turn golden. After the rice is harvested, it is milled to take away the inedible outer husk, revealing the next layer—the bran. Rice with its bran intact is brown rice. If the bran layer is also removed during the milling process, the result is white rice.

—

Cooked rice can be refrigerated in zipper-top plastic bags for up to 5 days or frozen for up to 2 months.

LONG-GRAIN RICE

Makes 4 cups/780 g

—

Long-grain rice is what is referred to as "dry-starch rice," meaning that when cooked, the long, thin grains remain distinct. Basmati and jasmine are long-grain varieties.

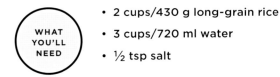

WHAT YOU'LL NEED

- 2 cups/430 g long-grain rice
- 3 cups/720 ml water
- ½ tsp salt

Place the rice in a sieve and rinse under a steady stream of cool water, stirring the grains. When the water runs clear, stop rinsing and shake the sieve to drain off excess water.

Combine the rice, 3 cups/720 ml water, and salt in a medium rice cooker, cover, and set it to the regular cycle. After cooking, allow the rice to continue steaming for an additional 10 minutes on the keep-warm setting or with the machine turned off. (Many rice cookers, including all fuzzy-logic machines, do this automatically.) Fluff the rice and serve.

—

COOK'S NOTE: *With a basic machine, the ambient heat in the rice cooker will keep it warm for about 30 minutes without overcooking it. An on/off/warm machine will keep the rice warm for about 45 minutes after it has finished cooking, and a fuzzy-logic machine will keep the rice warm even longer.*

MEDIUM-GRAIN RICE

Makes 2 cups/390 g

———

Medium-grain rice contains more starch than long-grain. Use this type of rice for risotto and paella. Arborio rice is a popular medium-grain rice (sometimes mistaken for short-grain), but my favorites are Vialone Nano and Carnaroli.

If you would like to serve medium-grain rice plain, rather than in a risotto or paella, these are the proportions. A drizzle of extra-virgin olive oil and some chopped fresh herbs added at the end will make this a great dish to serve with grilled meats, poultry, or seafood.

WHAT YOU'LL NEED

- 1 cup/215 g medium-grain rice
- 3 cups/720 ml water or broth (see Cook's Note)
- 1 tsp salt

Place the rice in a sieve and rinse under a steady stream of cool water, stirring the grains. When the water runs clear, stop rinsing and shake the sieve to drain off excess water.

Combine the rice, 3 cups/720 ml water, and salt in a medium rice cooker. Cover and set to the regular cycle. After cooking, allow the rice to continue steaming for an additional 10 minutes on the keep-warm setting or with the machine turned off. (Many rice cookers, including all fuzzy-logic machines, do this automatically.) Fluff the rice and serve.

———

COOK'S NOTE: *The choice of broth or water is up to the cook. Vegetable, chicken, beef, or seafood broths can be used; choose the one that will complement the food you are serving with the rice.*

SHORT-GRAIN RICE

Makes 4 cups/780 g

—

Short-grain rice is round in appearance and high in starch. When cooked, the grains stick together, like sushi rice. The proportions are generally one part rice to one part liquid.

WHAT YOU'LL NEED

- 2 cups/430 g short-grain rice
- 2 cups/480 ml water or broth (see Cook's Note, facing page)
- 1 tsp salt

Place the rice in a sieve and rinse under a steady stream of cool water, stirring the grains. When the water runs clear, stop rinsing and shake the sieve to drain off excess water.

Combine the rice, 2 cups/480 ml water, and salt in a medium rice cooker. Cover and set to the regular cycle. After cooking, allow the rice to continue steaming for an additional 10 minutes on the keep-warm setting or with the machine turned off. (Many rice cookers, including all fuzzy-logic machines, do this automatically.) Fluff the rice and serve.

BROWN RICE

Makes 4 cups/780 g

———

A bit chewier and nuttier tasting than its white cousins, brown rice is delicious in a pilaf or served as a side dish. It's a great grain to add to your family's diet.

WHAT YOU'LL NEED

- 2 cups/430 g short-, medium-, or long-grain brown rice
- 3¾ cups/900 ml water or broth (see Cook's Note, page 20)
- 1 tsp salt

Place the rice in a sieve and rinse under a steady stream of cool water, stirring the grains. When the water runs clear, stop rinsing and shake the sieve to drain off excess water.

Combine the rice, 3¾ cups/900 ml water, and salt in a medium rice cooker. Cover and set to the regular cycle. After cooking, allow the rice to continue steaming for an additional 10 minutes on the keep-warm setting or with the machine turned off. (Many rice cookers, including all fuzzy-logic machines, do this automatically.) Fluff the rice and serve.

WILD RICE

Makes 2½ cups/570 g

I love to cook wild rice and then freeze the leftovers in 1-cup/230-g packages to add to soups and side dishes.

WHAT YOU'LL NEED

- 1 cup/215 g wild rice
- 2½ cups/600 ml water or broth (see Cook's Note, page 20)
- 1 tsp salt

Place the rice in a sieve and rinse under a steady stream of cool water, stirring the grains. When the water runs clear, stop rinsing and shake the sieve to drain off excess water.

Combine the rice, 2½ cups/600 ml water, and salt in a medium rice cooker. Cover and set to the regular cycle. After cooking, allow the rice to continue steaming for an additional 10 minutes on the keep-warm setting or with the machine turned off. (Many rice cookers, including all fuzzy-logic machines, do this automatically.) Fluff the rice and serve.

ABOUT WILD RICE

Wild rice is not rice at all, but the seed of an aquatic grass that was first harvested by Native Americans in the far northern areas of the United States. The state grain of Minnesota, wild rice is high in protein, fiber, B vitamins, and minerals. It can be used in a variety of different ways—in soups, casseroles, and salads; as a stuffing for small game hens; and cooked like a pilaf for a delicious side dish. Now grown in Northern California as well as in the Great Lakes region, wild rice has a crunchy, pleasant bite.

Cooked wild rice can be stored in the refrigerator for up to 4 days or in the freezer for up to 2 months.

BULGUR

Makes 2 cups/460 g

Simply drizzled with some extra-virgin olive oil and a squeeze of lemon, plain bulgur is a delicious and wholesome side dish when served with steamed fish or chicken. Or it can be made into a pilaf like Black Kale, Winter Squash, and Bulgur Pilaf (page 151).

WHAT YOU'LL NEED

- 1 cup/215 g medium-grain bulgur
- 2 cups/480 ml water or broth (see Cook's Note, page 20)
- 1 tsp salt

Place the bulgur in a sieve and rinse under a steady stream of cool water, stirring the grains. When the water runs clear, stop rinsing and shake the sieve to drain off excess water.

Combine the bulgur, 2 cups/480 ml water, and salt in a medium rice cooker. Cover and set to the regular cycle. After cooking, fluff the bulgur and serve hot.

BULGUR BREAKFAST PORRIDGE

—

Coat the inside of a medium rice cooker with nonstick cooking spray. Replace the water with milk and combine with the bulgur and salt in the rice cooker. Cover and set to the regular cycle. Set a timer for 20 minutes. When the timer goes off, the bulgur should be tender, with some milk left in the cooker. You may need to add more milk if the bulgur is very sticky. Serve the porridge warm.

ABOUT BULGUR

When wheat kernels are steamed, dried, and crushed, the result is bulgur. It takes a short time to cook and comes in fine and medium (or coarse) grain. Tabbouleh, the familiar Middle Eastern salad, is made with fine bulgur. High in protein and fiber, bulgur is a great substitute for rice or other grains in soup, salad, pilaf, and cereal.

—

*Cooked bulgur can be stored in the refrigerator for up to 4 days
or in the freezer for up to 1 month.*

FARRO

Makes 2 cups/330 g

———

Farro comes pearled (with the bran removed) and whole grain. Pearled farro will take a shorter amount of time to cook. Cooked farro is delicious served as a side dish with a drizzle of extra-virgin olive oil and a sprinkle of chopped fresh herbs. Toss it into soups and stews in place of another starch or use it as a stuffing for meats, vegetables, and poultry. You can also use cooled farro to make a salad, as you would rice.

WHAT YOU'LL NEED

- 1 cup/200 g farro (pearled or whole grain)
- 1⅔ cups/405 ml water or broth (see Cook's Note, page 20)
- 1 tsp salt

Place the farro in a sieve and rinse under a steady stream of cool water, stirring the grains. When the water runs clear, stop rinsing and shake the sieve to drain off excess water.

Combine the farro, 1⅔ cups/405 ml water, and salt in a medium rice cooker. Cover and set to the regular cycle. After cooking, allow the farro to continue steaming for an additional 5 minutes on the keep-warm setting or with the machine turned off. (Many rice cookers, including all fuzzy-logic machines, do this automatically.) Fluff the farro and serve.

FARRO BREAKFAST PORRIDGE

—

Coat the inside of a medium rice cooker with nonstick cooking spray. Combine 1 cup/200 g pearled farro, 1²⁄₃ cups/405 ml milk, 1 cup/240 ml water, and 1 tsp salt in the rice cooker. Cover and set to the regular cycle. Set a timer for 20 minutes. When the timer goes off, the farro should be very tender. If not, cover and cook for another 5 to 10 minutes. The porridge should look like liquidy risotto, with bits of the farro and milky broth. Serve the porridge warm.

ABOUT FARRO

Farro is an ancient grain, sometimes mistakenly called "emmer wheat" or spelt, but it is neither; it is farro—what the Roman legions ate to sustain their energy. Farro is a low-gluten-index grain that is high in fiber, magnesium, and vitamins. And it's easy to digest. Similar in texture to Arborio rice, farro makes dishes creamier and thicker, but it does not become gummy like rice.

—

Cooked farro can be stored in the refrigerator for up to 5 days or in the freezer for up to 2 months.

QUINOA

Makes 2 cups/460 g

———

Quinoa (pronounced KEEN-wah*) is a small seed that, when cooked, makes a great host for spicy ingredients. It's a gluten-free source of plant protein as well as antioxidants and minerals such as iron and magnesium. Quinoa is delicious as a side dish or as a stuffing for vegetables, and it is also a great addition to summer salads. Look for quinoa in bulk bins at your local health food store, rather than in packages at the grocer, as it will be fresher. Also look for quinoa that has been prewashed. If it has not been washed, then it will need a good rinsing before you add it to the rice cooker. (I like to wash prewashed, too, to get rid of the bitter outer coating and any leftover hulls.)*

WHAT YOU'LL NEED

- 1½ cups/280 g quinoa
- 2¼ cups/540 ml water or broth (see Cook's Note, page 20)
- 1 tsp salt

If the quinoa has not been prewashed, place it in a fine-mesh sieve and rinse with cold water, stirring the quinoa. When the water runs clear and any bits of hull have risen to the top, discard the hulls. (If the quinoa has been prewashed, just give it a quick rinse.)

Combine the quinoa, 2¼ cups/540 ml water, and salt in a medium rice cooker. Cover and set to the regular cycle. After cooking, allow the quinoa to continue steaming for an additional 5 minutes on the keep-warm setting or with the machine turned off. (Many rice cookers, including all fuzzy-logic machines, do this automatically.) Serve hot, or allow to cool and use in salads.

BARLEY

Makes 2½ cups/570 g

—

Barley, a good source of fiber, calcium, and iron, is a great grain to slip into your family's diet. Barley salads are some of my all-time favorites for summer entertaining. Barley can be used interchangeably with farro or bulgur, but it has a tendency to thicken stews and soups, so a word to the wise: it will suck up extra liquid. I buy pearled barley, which cooks more quickly than unpearled.

WHAT YOU'LL NEED

- 1 cup/130 g pearled barley
- 2¼ cups/540 ml broth or water (see Cook's Note, page 20)

Place the barley in a sieve and rinse under a steady stream of cool water, stirring the grains. When the water runs clear, stop rinsing and shake the sieve to drain off excess water.

Combine the barley and broth in a medium rice cooker. Cover and set to the regular cycle. After cooking, allow the barley to continue steaming for an additional 5 minutes on the keep-warm setting or with the machine turned off. (Many rice cookers, including all fuzzy-logic machines, do this automatically.) Serve hot, or allow to cool and use in salads.

GRITS

Makes 3 cups/685 g

———

Many of us are familiar with the instant variety of grits, which are about as tasty as wallpaper paste. But cook up a batch of stone-ground grits, and your family will ask for them every night! The texture and flavor of stone-ground grits is far superior to the instant version, so look for them in your supermarket or natural food store. I especially like to serve grits with over-easy eggs for a lumberjack's breakfast or with spicy shrimp (see page 105) over the top for dinner.

WHAT YOU'LL NEED

- 1 cup/140 g coarse stone-ground grits
- 2¾ to 3¼ cups/660 to 780 ml water or broth (see Cook's Note)
- 1 tsp salt
- 2 Tbsp unsalted butter
- 2 or 3 dashes hot sauce

Combine the grits, 2¾ cups/660 ml of the water, and the salt in a medium rice cooker. Cover and set to the regular cycle. During the cycle (which may take up to 30 minutes), stir the grits a few times. If the grits become thick and are beginning to stick to the bottom of the pan, stir in a bit more of the water toward the end of the cooking time. After cooking, stir in the butter and hot sauce. Serve hot.

———

COOK'S NOTE: *If you would like creamy grits, use 1½ cups/360 ml whole milk and 1¼ cups/300 ml water or broth.*

POLENTA

Makes 4 cups/915 g

—

My Italian nonna made polenta once in a blue moon. Because of the endless stirring and hours of cooking involved, she would only make it when her children or grandchildren begged her. We knew that it would be absolutely delicious and that the pork ragu served on top would be out of this world.

With a rice cooker, you can be on your way to polenta perfection in the time it takes to organize the ingredients. You will want to use stone-ground coarse cornmeal—this gives the dish some character and lots of flavor.

WHAT YOU'LL NEED

- 1 cup/140 g Italian coarse-grain cornmeal or polenta (see Cook's Note)

- 4 cups/960 ml water or vegetable broth (see Cook's Note, page 20)

- 1 tsp salt

Coat the inside of a medium rice cooker with nonstick cooking spray. Add the polenta, water, and salt and stir to combine. Cover and set to the regular cycle. During the cycle, stir occasionally (and add more water if the polenta is sticking to the pot). Serve hot.

—

COOK'S NOTE: *Avoid instant polenta, which won't cook properly in the rice cooker.*

OATMEAL

Makes 3 cups/685 g

—

Steel-cut oats are all the rage at trendy breakfast places. Your rice cooker will make perfect oatmeal every time and keep it warm for late risers.

WHAT YOU'LL NEED

- 1 cup/85 g steel-cut oats
- 1½ cups/360 ml whole milk
- 1 cup/240 ml water
- ½ tsp salt

Coat the inside of a medium rice cooker with nonstick cooking spray. Add the oats, milk, water, and salt and stir to combine. Cover and set to the regular cycle, or to the porridge cycle on fuzzy-logic models. (Check midway through the cooking cycle to make sure it is not running out of liquid and add more if necessary.) After cooking, switch to the warm cycle or turn the machine off and keep covered until you are ready to serve.

DRIED BEANS

Makes 2½ to 3 cups/570 to 685 g

___

All dried beans need to be soaked before cooking in a rice cooker so that they end up creamy and tender. You can soak them overnight as described in the following recipe, or for a quick-soak method, see the Cook's Note.

This basic recipe works well for a variety of beans: try red beans, pinto beans, cannellini (large white beans), or black beans. All are great sources of protein and can be part of a main dish or side dish, or tossed into soups and salads.

WHAT YOU'LL NEED

- 1 cup/200 g dried beans, picked over
- 4 cups/960 ml water
- ¼ cup/60 ml extra-virgin olive oil (optional)
- Salt and freshly ground black pepper (optional)

In a bowl, cover the beans with 1 in/2.5 cm of water. Let soak overnight at room temperature.

Drain the beans and combine them with the 4 cups/960 ml water in a medium rice cooker. Cover, set to the regular cycle, and cook until the rice cooker shuts off automatically; this will take about 1½ hours. Drain the beans. Toss with the olive oil and season with salt and pepper, if desired, before serving.

___

COOK'S NOTE: *To quick-soak dried beans, in a medium saucepan, cover the beans with 1 in/2.5 cm water. Bring to a boil over medium-high heat, turn the heat to low, and simmer, uncovered, for 2 minutes. Remove the pan from the heat, cover, and let the beans soak for 1 hour. Drain the beans and cook in the rice cooker as directed.*

Do not add salt to the water; it will toughen the skins of some types of beans.

APPLESAUCE

Makes 3 to 4 cups/720 to 960 ml

——

While writing this book, I realized that the rice cooker would be perfect for making applesauce and other fruit sauces in small batches. The best apples for sauce are softer varieties that don't hold a lot of water, such as Jonathan, Golden Delicious, Cortland, Ambrosia, Braeburn, Cameo, Pink Lady, Jazz, and Gala.

WHAT YOU'LL NEED

- 4 cups/600 g peeled, cored, and coarsely chopped cooking apples
- ¼ cup/60 ml apple cider or apple juice, plus more if needed
- 1 Tbsp fresh lemon juice
- 1 cup/200 g sugar, plus more if needed
- 1 tsp ground cinnamon, plus more if needed
- ⅛ tsp ground nutmeg, plus more if needed

Combine the apples, apple cider, lemon juice, sugar, cinnamon, and nutmeg in a medium rice cooker, stirring to blend. Cover, set to the regular cycle, and set a timer for 30 minutes. Stir every 10 minutes to make sure there is enough liquid and the sauce isn't sticking to the bottom. If necessary, add a little more cider. After cooking, using either an immersion blender or a regular blender, purée the applesauce. Taste for seasoning and adjust by adding more sugar, cinnamon, or nutmeg. Cool, cover, and refrigerate for up to 1 month.

STONE FRUIT SAUCE

Makes 3½ to 4 cups/840 to 960 ml

——

During stone fruit season, I tend to get carried away at the farmers' market. The intoxicating smells of peaches, nectarines, plums, and other stone fruits that come in during the summer overwhelm me, so we always have more than we can eat. This simple sauce is delicious on toast or a bagel, or you can spoon it over ice cream or pound cake for a simple dessert.

WHAT YOU'LL NEED

- 4 cups/600 g peeled, pitted, and coarsely chopped stone fruit (peaches, nectarines, plums, or a combination)
- ¼ cup/60 ml peach nectar, plus more if needed
- 2 Tbsp fresh lemon juice, plus more if needed
- 2 tsp vanilla paste
- Sugar (optional)

Combine the stone fruit, peach nectar, lemon juice, and vanilla paste in a medium rice cooker, stirring to blend. Cover, set to the regular cycle, and set a timer for 30 minutes. Stir every 10 minutes to make sure there is enough liquid and the sauce isn't sticking to the bottom. If necessary, add a little more peach nectar. After cooking, using either an immersion blender or a regular blender, purée the sauce. Taste for seasoning and adjust by adding sugar or more lemon juice. Cool, cover, and refrigerate for up to 1 month.

POULTRY

CHICKEN MISO SOUP WITH OYSTER MUSHROOMS AND GREENS

Comfort food for the soul, this soup, fragrant with ginger and miso and loaded with noodles and greens, is a great warm-up on a cold day. If you have leftover rotisserie chicken, the soup is a snap to make; and with the rice cooker, there is only one pot to wash—a bonus in my book!

WHAT YOU'LL NEED

- 1 tsp soy sauce
- 2 boneless, skinless chicken breast halves (5 to 6 oz/140 to 170 g each), cut into bite-size pieces
- ½ lb/225 g oyster or shiitake mushrooms, finely chopped (remove stems from shiitakes)
- 3 green onions, white and tender green parts finely chopped and darker green parts thinly sliced for garnish
- 1 tsp grated peeled fresh ginger

- ½ cup/115 g white (shiro) miso (see Cook's Note, page 40)
- 4 cups/960 ml chicken or vegetable broth
- 2 cups/280 g finely chopped greens, such as bok choy, Napa cabbage, or spinach
- 8 oz/225 g cooked fresh Asian-style thin wheat noodles (see Cook's Note, page 40) or cooked thin pasta strands
- Toasted sesame oil for garnish

Set a medium rice cooker to the regular cycle or to quick cook if it's a fuzzy-logic machine. In a medium bowl, pour the soy sauce over the chicken and stir to coat the chicken. Transfer to the rice cooker and cook until the chicken is opaque on all sides (it will cook through in the soup). Remove the chicken to a plate. Add the mushrooms and chopped green onions to the rice cooker and cook for 3 to 4 minutes, until the mushrooms soften. Return the chicken to the cooker and add the ginger. In a large measuring cup, whisk the miso and chicken broth together and pour into the rice cooker. Add the greens.

Cover the rice cooker and reset to the regular cycle. Set a timer for 15 minutes. When the timer goes off, lift the cover and add the noodles, stirring to break them up. Cover and cook for another 2 minutes to warm the noodles. Serve the soup garnished with a few drops of sesame oil and the reserved sliced green onion tops.

continued

——

COOK'S NOTE: *White miso is milder than darker miso, which makes it more kid friendly. And it's so good for you and your kids. It will keep in the fridge for up to 1 year.*

The noodles included in yakisoba kits sold in the refrigerator section of well-stocked grocery stores are ideal for this recipe. They are precooked so they can be used straight from the package; discard the seasoning packets that are included with the noodles.

This soup lends itself to many variations. Substitute leftover shrimp, pork, or beef for the chicken and replace the greens with other vegetables, such as finely chopped broccoli, zucchini, snow peas, or any leftover vegetables from a previous dinner. If you would prefer to omit the broth, substitute water and proceed as directed.

LEMON CHICKEN SOUP
WITH ORZO

Fragrant with the zesty aroma of lemon and filled with tender chicken and orzo pasta, this soup will fill your rice cooker with a little bit of the Mediterranean. This is just the thing to warm your family on a hectic weeknight. It's also a great way to use up leftover chicken from a previous meal.

WHAT YOU'LL NEED

- 1 Tbsp extra-virgin olive oil
- 1 leek, white part only, finely chopped
- 2 celery ribs, finely chopped
- Grated zest and juice of 1 lemon, plus thin slices of lemon for garnish (see Cook's Note)
- 4 cups/960 ml chicken broth

- ½ cup/100 g orzo
- 2 cups/280 g finely chopped cooked chicken
- Salt and freshly ground black pepper (optional)
- Sprigs of fresh flat-leaf parsley for garnish

Set a medium rice cooker to the regular cycle or to quick cook if it's a fuzzy-logic machine. Heat the olive oil and sauté the leek, celery, and lemon zest for 2 to 3 minutes, until the leek begins to soften. Add the chicken broth, orzo, and chopped chicken to the pot.

Cover the rice cooker and reset to the regular cycle. Set a timer for 15 minutes. When the timer goes off, check the orzo; it should be tender. If not, cover and cook for another 5 minutes. Season with salt and pepper if needed. Stir in the lemon juice and serve in soup bowls, garnished with a slice of lemon and a sprig of parsley.

COOK'S NOTE: *Make sure to wash citrus thoroughly with hot water and a vegetable scrubber. Citrus fruits are waxed for shipping, and the wax, if not washed off, will give your food a greasy coating.*

SPICY CHICKEN AND BROWN BASMATI RICE LETTUCE WRAPS

Fragrant with garlic, ginger, and soy, these lettuce wraps include a bit of brown basmati rice to give you a hearty dinner dish. Although Asian wraps are most often served with iceberg lettuce, butterhead lettuce makes a nice substitute here. If you make the sauce, pass it separately so each diner can drizzle it on the lettuce wraps.

WHAT YOU'LL NEED

- 2 boneless, skinless chicken breast halves (5 to 6 oz/140 to 170 g each), cut into ½-in/12-mm pieces
- ¼ cup/60 ml soy sauce
- 2 Tbsp mirin (Japanese sweet rice wine)
- 1 Tbsp hoisin sauce
- 3 or 4 dashes Sriracha (optional)
- ½ cup/110 g brown basmati rice
- 2 Tbsp vegetable oil
- 2 garlic cloves, minced

- 1 tsp grated peeled fresh ginger
- One 8-oz/225-g can water chestnuts, drained and finely chopped
- ¾ cup/180 ml chicken or vegetable broth
- 1 Tbsp toasted sesame oil
- 2 green onions, white and tender green parts, finely chopped
- 1 head iceberg or butterhead lettuce, leaves separated
- Sweet and Spicy Soy Sauce (recipe follows) for serving (optional)

In a medium bowl, combine the chicken, soy sauce, mirin, hoisin, and Sriracha (if using), stirring to coat the chicken. Set aside.

Place the rice in a sieve and rinse under a steady stream of cool water, stirring the grains. When the water runs clear, stop rinsing and shake the sieve to drain off excess water.

Set a medium rice cooker to the regular cycle or to quick cook if it's a fuzzy-logic machine. Heat the vegetable oil, add the garlic and ginger, and sauté for 1 minute, or until fragrant. Add the chicken and marinade and cook, stirring, until the chicken turns white on all sides (it will cook through with the rice). Add the water chestnuts and rice, stirring to coat the rice. Stir in the chicken broth.

Cover the rice cooker and reset to the regular cycle, or to mixed cook if it's a fuzzy-logic machine. When the rice is finished cooking, stir in the sesame oil and green onions. Transfer to a serving bowl. Pass the lettuce leaves separately for each diner to wrap their own, along with the sweet and spicy soy sauce, if desired.

SWEET AND SPICY SOY SAUCE

MAKES ¼ CUP/60 ML

When served at restaurants, the lettuce wraps are drizzled with this sauce. It also makes a terrific dip for gyoza or steamed dumplings.

WHAT YOU'LL NEED

- 2 Tbsp soy sauce, plus more if needed
- 1 tsp sugar
- 1 Tbsp mirin (Japanese sweet rice wine)
- 3 dashes Sriracha, plus more if needed

- 1 garlic clove, minced
- 1 tsp toasted sesame oil
- 1 green onion, white and tender green parts, finely chopped

In a small bowl, whisk together the soy sauce, sugar, mirin, Sriracha, garlic, sesame oil, and green onion. Taste for seasoning and add more Sriracha or soy sauce as needed. Store in the refrigerator for up to 4 days.

THAI-INSPIRED CHICKEN AND RICE LETTUCE WRAPS WITH SPICY MANGO RELISH

—

Thai chicken with basil is one of my daughter's favorite weeknight meals. The rice cooker makes it simple, and it's economical, too. The chicken cooks with jasmine rice and is rolled in butterhead lettuce leaves, drizzled with a bit of sauce, and topped with chopped basil, cilantro, bean sprouts, and green onions. Think of it as an Asian soft taco. Thai chiles are very hot, so use them sparingly if your family isn't fond of spicy food.

WHAT YOU'LL NEED

- ½ cup/110 g jasmine rice
- 2 Tbsp vegetable oil
- 3 garlic cloves, minced
- ½ cup/80 g finely diced shallots
- 1 to 2 green or red Thai chiles, stemmed and finely chopped
- 1½ lb/680 g boneless, skinless chicken breast, cut into small pieces, or 1½ lb/680 g ground chicken or turkey
- 2 Tbsp fish sauce
- 1 Tbsp soy sauce
- 1 tsp rice vinegar
- 1 Tbsp sugar

- 1½ cups/360 ml chicken or vegetable broth
- 1 butterhead lettuce, leaves separated
- ½ cup/30 g tightly packed basil leaves, finely chopped, plus additional whole or sliced leaves
- ½ cup/30 g chopped fresh cilantro
- 3 green onions, white and tender green parts, finely chopped
- ½ cup/25 g bean sprouts
- Spicy Mango Relish (page 47) for serving (optional)

Place the rice in a sieve and rinse under a steady stream of cool water, stirring the grains. When the water runs clear, stop rinsing and shake the sieve to drain off excess water.

continued

Set a medium rice cooker to the regular cycle or to quick cook if it's a fuzzy-logic machine. Heat the vegetable oil, add the garlic and shallots, and sauté for 1 minute, or until fragrant. Add the chiles and continue sautéing for 2 to 3 minutes, until the chiles begin to soften. Add the chicken and sauté until it is no longer pink in color, breaking up the clumps if ground. If there is excess water in the pan, drain a bit of it. Add the fish sauce, soy sauce, rice vinegar, and sugar. Stir to blend. Stir the rice into the chicken mixture and pour in the chicken broth.

Cover the rice cooker and reset to the regular cycle. At the end of the cycle, stir the chicken and rice mixture. Re-cover and continue steaming for an additional 10 minutes on the keep-warm setting or with the machine turned off. (Many rice cookers, including all fuzzy-logic machines, do this automatically.) Mound the chicken and rice in a serving bowl. Put the lettuce, basil, cilantro, green onions, and bean sprouts in separate bowls and let each diner create his or her own soft taco. Serve with the mango relish, if desired.

SPICY MANGO RELISH

MAKES ½ CUP/90 G

This sauce is a delicious accompaniment to lettuce wraps and other spicy foods. Fresh mangoes are available most of the year in full-service markets. Look for mangoes that are soft to the touch or are beginning to soften. Leave them on the counter to further soften and use a serrated peeler to peel them.

WHAT YOU'LL NEED

- 1 tsp finely chopped red Thai chile
- 2 Tbsp finely chopped red onion
- 2 garlic cloves, minced
- 1 tsp finely grated peeled fresh ginger
- 3 Tbsp fish sauce

- 1 Tbsp soy sauce
- 1 Tbsp fresh lime juice
- 2 tsp sugar
- 1 large mango, peeled and finely chopped

In a medium mixing bowl, combine the chile, red onion, garlic, ginger, fish sauce, soy sauce, lime juice, and sugar, whisking to dissolve the sugar. Add the mango and toss until blended. Cover and refrigerate for up to 3 days.

CABBAGE LEAVES STUFFED WITH FRUITED BROWN RICE

—

Made with cooked brown rice and ground chicken or turkey, these stuffed cabbage leaves bubble away in a sweet and savory tomato sauce. They are a great way to use leftover rice. Mashed potatoes and applesauce are the perfect side dishes.

WHAT YOU'LL NEED

- 8 large outer leaves of 1 head green cabbage (save the rest for another use)
- 2 Tbsp extra-virgin olive oil
- 1 large onion, finely chopped
- One 28-oz/795-g can crushed tomatoes, with their juice
- 2 Tbsp cider vinegar
- 2 Tbsp sugar

- 1 lb/455 g ground chicken or turkey
- 1½ cups/295 g cold cooked brown rice (see page 22)
- ¼ cup/15 g finely chopped fresh flat-leaf parsley
- ¼ cup/40 g golden raisins or dried apricots, chopped
- 1 large egg
- Salt and freshly ground black pepper

Arrange the cabbage leaves on a microwavable plate and cover with a moistened paper towel. Microwave on high for 1 minute and 30 seconds, remove from the microwave, and allow to cool. The cabbage should just be pliable. If you don't have a microwave, put the cabbage in a large colander and pour boiling water over it.

Set a medium rice cooker to the regular cycle or to quick cook if it's a fuzzy-logic machine. Heat the olive oil, add half the onion, and sauté for 2 to 3 minutes, or until fragrant. Stir in the tomatoes, cider vinegar, and sugar. Cover and bring to a simmer.

In a large bowl, combine the chicken, rice, remaining chopped onion, parsley, raisins, egg, 1 tsp salt, and ½ tsp pepper, mixing well to combine the ingredients.

continued

Lay the cabbage leaves on a work surface. Place 2 to 3 Tbsp of the chicken mixture (this will vary depending on the size of the leaf) near the core end of a leaf. Roll up the leaf, folding in the sides as you roll to form a package. Repeat with the remaining cabbage leaves and chicken mixture. Arrange the rolls in the sauce in the rice cooker.

Cover the rice cooker and reset to the regular cycle. Set a timer for 30 minutes. When the timer goes off, make sure that the chicken is cooked through (an instant-read thermometer inserted into a cabbage leaf should register 165°F/74°C). Season with salt and pepper, if needed. Serve the cabbage rolls warm.

SPINACH RICE WITH CHICKEN, PANCETTA, AND CORN

This delicious rice dish combines some of my favorite ingredients—bright green spinach, sweet corn, chicken, and salty pancetta—along with brown basmati rice for a tasty main dish.

WHAT YOU'LL NEED

- 2 cups/430 g brown basmati or other long-grain rice
- 2 Tbsp extra-virgin olive oil
- One ½-in-/12-mm-thick slice pancetta, finely diced
- 1 garlic clove, minced
- ½ cup/80 g finely chopped sweet yellow onion, such as Vidalia
- 2 boneless, skinless chicken breast halves (5 to 6 oz/140 to 170 g each), cut into bite-size pieces
- 2 cups/340 g corn kernels, cut fresh from the cob, or frozen kernels (don't defrost)
- 3 cups/720 ml chicken or vegetable broth
- 2 cups/280 g packed baby spinach, coarsely chopped

Place the rice in a sieve and rinse under a steady stream of cool water, stirring the grains. When the water runs clear, stop rinsing and shake the sieve to drain off excess water.

Set a medium rice cooker to the regular cycle or to quick cook if it's a fuzzy-logic machine. Heat the olive oil, add the pancetta, and sauté until it becomes crispy. Add the garlic and onion and sauté for another 3 minutes, or until the onion is softened. Add the chicken and sauté until the chicken is white on all sides. Add the corn and rice and stir to combine. Gradually add the chicken broth.

Cover the rice cooker and reset to the regular cycle. At the end of the cycle, stir in the spinach. Re-cover and continue steaming for an additional 5 minutes on the keep-warm setting or with the machine turned off. (Many rice cookers, including all fuzzy-logic machines, do this automatically.) Serve warm.

SPINACH-WRAPPED CHICKEN OVER BROWN RICE PILAF WITH SOY DIPPING SAUCE

Here's another simple dish to serve during the week. The chicken is marinated in soy, ginger, and garlic and then wrapped in spinach leaves to steam above a brown rice pilaf. Marinate the chicken in the morning, and you will be ready to cook the dish when you arrive home. A salty and sweet dipping sauce for the chicken complements the entire dish.

WHAT YOU'LL NEED

Chicken

- 4 boneless, skinless chicken breast halves (5 to 6 oz/140 to 170 g each)
- ½ cup/120 ml soy sauce
- ¼ cup/60 ml mirin (Japanese sweet rice wine)
- 2 Tbsp sugar
- 2 garlic cloves, minced
- 1 tsp grated peeled fresh ginger
- 1 lb/455 g large spinach leaves, tough stems removed

Rice and Edamame

- 2 cups/430 g brown rice
- 1 Tbsp vegetable oil
- 1 medium onion, finely chopped
- 3¾ cups/900 ml chicken or vegetable broth
- 1 cup/170 g frozen shelled edamame, thawed

Dipping Sauce

- ¾ cup/180 ml soy sauce
- 2 Tbsp toasted sesame oil
- 1 Tbsp rice vinegar
- 1 tsp grated peeled fresh ginger
- 1 garlic clove, minced
- ¼ cup/50 g sugar
- 2 green onions, white and tender green parts, thinly sliced on the diagonal
- 2 Tbsp toasted sesame seeds

TO MAKE THE CHICKEN: Place the chicken into a large zipper-top plastic bag. In a small bowl, whisk together the soy sauce, mirin, sugar, garlic, and ginger. Pour the marinade over the chicken, seal the bag, and marinate for at least 2 hours, or up to 8 hours, in the refrigerator.

Arrange the spinach leaves on a microwavable plate and cover with a moistened paper towel. Microwave on high for 20 seconds, just to soften the spinach. If you don't have a microwave, put the spinach in a colander and pour boiling water over it. Drain the marinade and pat the chicken dry with paper towels. Wrap each chicken breast in several spinach leaves, arrange in the steamer basket of the rice cooker, and set aside.

TO MAKE THE RICE AND EDAMAME: Place the rice in a sieve and rinse under a steady stream of cool water, stirring the grains. When the water runs clear, stop rinsing and shake the sieve to drain off excess water.

Set a medium rice cooker to the regular cycle or to quick cook if it's a fuzzy-logic machine. Heat the vegetable oil, add the onion, and sauté for 2 minutes, or until it begins to soften. Add the rice and cook for another 2 minutes, to toast the grains. Gradually stir in the chicken broth. Arrange the steamer basket over the rice.

Cover the rice cooker and reset to the regular cycle or to the brown-rice cycle on a fuzzy-logic machine. At the end of the cycle, check the chicken for doneness; it should register 165°F/74°C on an instant-read thermometer. Stir the rice and add the edamame. Re-cover and continue steaming for an additional 5 minutes on the keep-warm setting or with the machine turned off. (Many rice cookers, including all fuzzy-logic machines, do this automatically.)

MEANWHILE, MAKE THE DIPPING SAUCE: In a small bowl, combine the soy sauce, sesame oil, rice vinegar, ginger, garlic, sugar, and green onions, stirring to blend. Stir in the sesame seeds just before serving.

Remove the chicken from the steamer basket. Arrange the rice on a serving platter and top with the chicken. Drizzle some of the dipping sauce over the chicken and serve the rest on the side.

YAKITORI-INSPIRED CHICKEN WITH MUSHROOM-VEGETABLE RICE

Yakitori are skewers of chicken that are marinated and then grilled. In this adaptation, the chicken breasts are seared in a grill pan and steamed over rice, which is fragrant with the earthy aroma of shiitake mushrooms and enriched with shredded carrots and zucchini. It is delicious cold for lunch. This recipe works well with salmon or shrimp, too, so consider mixing things up a bit.

WHAT YOU'LL NEED

Chicken

- 4 boneless, skinless chicken breast halves (5 to 6 oz/140 to 170 g each)
- ¼ cup/60 ml soy sauce
- ½ cup/120 ml mirin (Japanese sweet rice wine)
- ¼ cup/50 g sugar
- 2 Tbsp ketchup
- 2 garlic cloves, minced
- 1 tsp grated peeled fresh ginger
- 1 Tbsp toasted sesame oil

Rice

- 2 cups/430 g long-grain rice
- 1 Tbsp vegetable oil
- 1 garlic clove, minced
- ½ lb/225 g shiitake mushrooms, stemmed and finely chopped
- 1 medium zucchini, coarsely grated
- 1 medium carrot, peeled and coarsely grated
- 2¾ cups/660 ml chicken or vegetable broth

- 2 green onions, white and tender green parts, finely chopped
- 1 Tbsp toasted sesame seeds

TO MAKE THE CHICKEN: Place the chicken breasts in a large zipper-top plastic bag. In a small bowl, whisk together the soy sauce, mirin, sugar, ketchup, garlic, ginger, and sesame oil. Pour the mixture over the chicken, seal the bag, and marinate the chicken in the refrigerator for at least 2 hours, or up to 8 hours. When ready to cook, drain the marinade into a small saucepan and boil gently for 5 minutes. Lower the heat and simmer until syrupy. Set aside for serving. Pat the chicken dry with paper towels. Heat a nonstick grill pan or skillet over medium-high heat and sear the chicken breasts on both sides, so that they have nice color. Arrange in the steamer basket and set aside.

TO MAKE THE RICE: Place the rice in a sieve and rinse under a steady stream of cool water, stirring the grains. When the water runs clear, stop rinsing and shake the sieve to drain off excess water.

Set a medium rice cooker to the regular cycle or to quick cook if it's a fuzzy-logic machine. Heat the vegetable oil, add the garlic and mushrooms, and sauté for about 3 minutes, or until the mushroom liquid begins to evaporate. Add the zucchini and carrot and sauté for another 1 minute. Stir in the rice and gradually add the chicken broth. Arrange the steamer basket over the rice.

Cover the rice cooker and reset to the regular cycle. While the rice and chicken are cooking, reheat the sauce so that it is warm when the rice is finished. At the end of the cycle, check the chicken for doneness; it should register 165°F/74°C on an instant-read thermometer. Stir the green onions into the rice and arrange on a large serving platter. Cut the chicken on the diagonal into thin strips and arrange over the rice. Drizzle some of the sauce over the chicken, sprinkle with the sesame seeds, and serve.

CHICKEN AND MUSHROOM RICE WITH SOY SAUCE AND GREEN ONIONS

In this simple dish, the chicken and vegetables cook with the rice and broth, resulting in comfort food to soothe a tired soul. And the dish is simple to put together, even on a busy weeknight. The secret is to cut all the meat and vegetables into small pieces. That way there are tasty nuggets throughout the rice.

WHAT YOU'LL NEED

- 1⅓ cups/285 g long-grain rice
- 2 Tbsp vegetable oil
- 1 garlic clove, minced
- ½ tsp finely grated peeled fresh ginger
- 1 boneless, skinless chicken breast half (5 to 6 oz/140 to 170 g), finely diced
- ½ lb/225 g cremini mushrooms, thinly sliced
- 1 medium carrot, peeled and coarsely grated
- 2 Tbsp soy sauce
- 2 cups/480 ml chicken or vegetable broth or water
- 2 green onions, white and tender green parts, finely chopped

Place the rice in a sieve and rinse under a steady stream of cool water, stirring the grains. When the water runs clear, stop rinsing and shake the sieve to drain off excess water.

Set a medium rice cooker to the regular cycle or to quick cook if it's a fuzzy-logic machine. Add the vegetable oil, garlic, and ginger and, when the oil begins to sputter, add the chicken. Sauté until the chicken is white on all sides (it will cook through during the cooking cycle). Add the mushrooms and continue to cook until they begin to soften. Add the carrot, soy sauce, rice, and chicken broth.

Cover the rice cooker and reset to the regular cycle or to mixed cook if it's a fuzzy-logic machine. At the end of the cooking cycle, the rice should be tender. Continue steaming for an additional 10 minutes on the keep-warm setting or with the machine turned off. (Many rice cookers, including all fuzzy-logic machines, do this automatically.) Fluff the rice, garnish with the green onions, and serve.

CURRIED CHICKEN AND RICE

Aromatic curry powder and creamy coconut milk transform chicken and rice into a luscious Southeast Asian dish that you can make on a weeknight. To make this a vegetarian dish, omit the chicken and replace with your favorite cut vegetables: chopped cauliflower, bell peppers, or zucchini. Peas, baby corn, or corn from the cob are good choices, too.

WHAT YOU'LL NEED

- 1½ cups/315 g long-grain rice
- 1 tsp vegetable oil
- 1 medium onion, finely chopped
- 1 medium tart apple, peeled, cored, and finely chopped
- 1 to 2 tsp curry powder
- 2 boneless, skinless chicken breast halves (5 to 6 oz/140 to 170 g each), cut into bite-size pieces
- 1½ cups/360 ml chicken or vegetable broth
- ½ cup/120 ml coconut milk

- ¼ cup/15 g finely chopped basil (Thai basil or dark opal basil are especially good)

Condiments

- Major Grey's chutney
- Chopped peanuts
- Cooked and crumbled bacon
- Finely chopped hard-cooked eggs
- Banana chips
- Finely chopped green onions
- Sriracha
- Shredded coconut

Place the rice in a sieve and rinse under a steady stream of cool water, stirring the grains. When the water runs clear, stop rinsing and shake the sieve to drain off excess water.

Set a medium rice cooker to the regular cycle or to quick cook if it's a fuzzy-logic machine. Heat the vegetable oil; add the onion, apple, and curry powder; and sauté for about 3 minutes or until the onion becomes translucent. Add the chicken and cook until white on all sides (it will cook through during the cooking cycle). Gently stir in the rice, chicken broth, and coconut milk.

Cover the rice cooker and reset to the regular cycle or to mixed cook if it's a fuzzy-logic machine. At the end of the cooking cycle, fluff the rice and sprinkle with the basil. Serve with the condiments on the side.

CHICKEN BIRYANI

Although typically associated with Indian cuisine, variations of biryani are served in many Asian countries, including Malaysia and Pakistan. For this adaptation, the chicken is marinated in yogurt and spices; sautéed with garlic, ginger, and onion; and then steamed along with basmati rice in the rice cooker. It's a great party dish, but it's simple enough for weeknights, too. Biryani generally uses about ten spices. I have found that biryani paste, sold at Indian grocers and online, is a great way to get this dish on the table quickly, and with lots of flavor.

WHAT YOU'LL NEED

- 1½ cups/360 ml plain yogurt
- 1 Tbsp biryani paste (Patak's is a good brand)
- 4 boneless, skinless chicken breast halves (5 to 6 oz/140 to 170 g each), cut into bite-size pieces
- 1½ cups/315 g basmati rice
- 1 Tbsp vegetable oil
- 1 medium onion, finely chopped
- 2 garlic cloves, minced
- 2 tsp grated peeled fresh ginger
- 2½ cups/600 ml chicken broth
- 1 cup/170 g golden raisins

In a large bowl, combine the yogurt and biryani paste. Add the chicken and stir to combine. Let the chicken marinate, covered, in the refrigerator for at least 2 hours, or up to 6 hours.

Place the rice in a sieve and rinse under a steady stream of cool water, stirring the grains. When the water runs clear, stop rinsing and shake the sieve to drain off excess water.

Set a medium rice cooker to the regular cycle or to quick cook if it's a fuzzy-logic machine. Heat the vegetable oil. Remove the chicken from the marinade with a slotted spoon, reserving the marinade. Pat the chicken dry with paper towels. In small batches, sauté the chicken until it turns white on all sides and remove to a plate. Add the onion, garlic, and ginger to the cooker and sauté for about 4 minutes, until the onion begins to turn translucent. Add the yogurt marinade to the cooker, cover, and bring to a boil. Return the chicken to the cooker and stir in the rice, chicken broth, and raisins.

Cover the rice cooker and reset to the regular cycle or to mixed cook if it's a fuzzy-logic machine. When the cooker turns off, fluff the rice and serve.

FILIPINO-STYLE CHICKEN ADOBO

When I visited the Philippines with my husband, I began to think that no one cooked anything but adobo—chicken or pork. I soon learned that every cook has her or his own way of making it and wants to impress their guests. For this rendition, you will need to cook the rice ahead of time and keep it warm until the adobo is finished. The requirements for this dish are soy sauce, garlic, vinegar, bay leaf, and black pepper—the other ingredients are left to the whim of the cook. The vinegar and soy combination tenderizes the meat and gives it a delicious sauce, which is perfect to serve over short-grain rice.

WHAT YOU'LL NEED

- ½ cup/120 ml soy sauce
- ½ cup/120 ml rice vinegar (see Cook's Note)
- 3 garlic cloves, minced
- 1 Tbsp grated peeled fresh ginger
- 1 large onion, finely chopped
- ½ tsp freshly ground black pepper

- 2 bay leaves
- 1 Tbsp vegetable oil
- 6 boneless, skinless chicken thighs
- 3 cups/585 g cooked short-grain rice (see page 21) for serving
- 4 green onions, white and tender green parts, finely chopped

In a small bowl, whisk together the soy sauce, rice vinegar, garlic, ginger, onion, black pepper, and bay leaves and set aside.

Set a medium rice cooker to the regular cycle or to quick cook if it's a fuzzy-logic machine. Heat the vegetable oil, add the chicken, and brown on all sides. Stir in the soy sauce mixture. Cover the rice cooker and reset to the regular cycle. Set a timer for 15 minutes. When the timer goes off, turn the chicken, re-cover, and cook for an additional 15 minutes. Check the chicken for doneness—it should be tender and cooked through. Serve the chicken over the rice and garnish with the green onions.

COOK'S NOTE: *Avoid seasoned rice vinegar, which contains sake, salt, and sugar; the amount of salt can be staggering. It's best to buy one that is pure rice vinegar. I like to use organic rice vinegar.*

SOUTHEAST ASIAN CHICKEN OVER COCONUT-PINEAPPLE RICE

In this chicken dish, the flavors of Southeast Asia are complemented by the delectable coconut-pineapple rice, giving you a taste of the tropics without a lot of fuss. The chicken is marinated in the sauce and then seared and steamed above the rice. I recommend using fresh pineapple, since the canned kind can disintegrate during the long cooking time. If canned is all you have, stir it in at the end and allow the rice to continue steaming for another 5 minutes. The flavor won't be as intense, but you will have discernible pineapple chunks in the rice.

WHAT YOU'LL NEED

Chicken

- 4 boneless, skinless chicken breast halves (5 to 6 oz/140 to 170 g each)
- 1 garlic clove, minced
- 1 tsp grated peeled fresh ginger
- ¼ tsp Sriracha
- ¼ cup/60 ml fish sauce
- 2 Tbsp firmly packed light brown sugar
- ¼ cup/60 ml coconut milk

Rice

- 2 cups/430 g long-grain rice
- 1 cup/240 ml water
- 1 cup/240 ml coconut milk
- 1 cup/240 ml pineapple juice
- 1½ cups/230 g chopped fresh pineapple

- 3 green onions, white and tender green parts, finely chopped
- 2 Tbsp finely chopped fresh mint
- Chopped pineapple for garnish

TO MAKE THE CHICKEN: Place the chicken breasts in a large zipper-top plastic bag. In a small bowl, whisk together the garlic, ginger, Sriracha, fish sauce, brown sugar, and coconut milk. Pour the mixture over the chicken in the bag and refrigerate for at least 2 hours, or up to 8 hours. Drain the marinade and pat the chicken dry with paper towels. Heat a large skillet over medium-high heat and sear the chicken on both sides to brown. Arrange the chicken in the steamer basket of the rice cooker and set aside.

continued

TO MAKE THE RICE: Place the rice in a sieve and rinse under a steady stream of cool water, stirring the grains. When the water runs clear, stop rinsing and shake the sieve to drain off excess water.

Transfer to a medium rice cooker and add the 1 cup/240 ml water, coconut milk, pineapple juice, and fresh pineapple, stirring well. Arrange the steamer basket on top of the rice.

Cover the rice cooker and set to the regular cycle or to quick cook if it's a fuzzy-logic machine. At the end of the cycle, check to make sure the chicken is cooked through. (It should register 165°F/74°C on an instant-read thermometer.) Re-cover and continue steaming for an additional 5 minutes on the keep-warm setting or with the machine turned off. (Many rice cookers, including all fuzzy-logic machines, do this automatically.) Cut the chicken on the diagonal into strips ½ in/12 mm thick. Fluff the rice, arrange on a serving platter, and arrange the chicken over the rice. Sprinkle with the green onions and mint and arrange any additional pineapple around the rim of the platter to serve.

ARROZ CON POLLO

—

It seems every South American and Central American country has some iteration of this chicken and rice dish. This one is my favorite, a combination of chicken, sweet Italian sausage, and vegetables, with savory notes from the cumin and turmeric, and a jolt from the chili powder. This is a great weeknight meal, since it just needs a quick sauté before adding the rice and beginning the rice machine's cooking cycle.

WHAT YOU'LL NEED

- 2 cups/430 g long-grain rice
- 2 Tbsp extra-virgin olive oil
- 3 boneless, skinless chicken breast halves (5 to 6 oz/140 to 170 g each), cut into ½-in/12-mm pieces
- ½ lb/225 g sweet Italian sausage, casing removed
- ½ cup/80 g finely chopped red onion
- 1 medium red bell pepper, cored, seeded, and finely chopped
- 2 garlic cloves, minced
- ½ tsp ground cumin

- ⅛ tsp chili powder
- ½ tsp ground turmeric
- One 14½-oz/415-g can chopped tomatoes, with their juice
- 1 bay leaf
- 1 cup/240 ml chicken or vegetable broth
- ¼ cup/15 g finely chopped fresh cilantro or flat-leaf parsley (see Cook's Note, page 65)

Place the rice in a sieve and rinse under a steady stream of cool water, stirring the grains. When the water runs clear, stop rinsing and shake the sieve to drain off excess water.

Set a medium rice cooker to the regular cycle or to quick cook if it's a fuzzy-logic machine. Heat the olive oil, add the chicken a few pieces at a time, and sauté until white on all sides. Remove the cooked chicken to a plate and continue to sauté until all the chicken is done. Add the sausage to the pan and sauté until it loses its pink color.

continued

Remove all but 1 Tbsp of fat from the pan. Add the onion, bell pepper, garlic, cumin, chili powder, and turmeric and sauté for 3 minutes, or until the vegetables begin to soften. Return the chicken to the pan and stir in the tomatoes, bay leaf, and rice. Gradually add the chicken broth.

Cover the rice cooker and reset to the regular cycle. At the end of the cooking cycle, stir the rice. Re-cover and continue steaming for an additional 5 minutes on the keep-warm setting or with the machine turned off. (Many rice cookers, including all fuzzy-logic machines, do this automatically.) Transfer the contents of the rice cooker to a large serving bowl and serve, garnished with the cilantro.

———

COOK'S NOTE: *Many people have an aversion to cilantro. You can use either flat-leaf parsley or cilantro for the garnish, whichever your family prefers.*

PORCINI-CRUSTED CHICKEN WITH BAROLO RISOTTO

—

This is just the dish to help you relive that visit to Tuscany: an elegant red risotto, redolent of rich Barolo wine, that cooks beneath the porcini-crusted chicken. The result is a succulent, moist chicken, with a flavorful risotto to serve alongside. Make sure to buy a good bottle of wine for this recipe. Otherwise, the risotto will have a distinctively winey flavor, which is difficult to correct. Younger Barolos tend to have a lot of tannin, so be careful when buying (see the Cook's Note).

WHAT YOU'LL NEED

Chicken

- ¼ cup/60 ml extra-virgin olive oil
- 1 tsp salt
- ½ tsp freshly ground black pepper
- ½ cup/100 g dried porcini mushrooms, crushed in the palm of your hand
- 4 boneless, skinless chicken breast halves (5 to 6 oz/140 to 170 g each)

Risotto

- 1 cup/215 g medium-grain rice, such as Arborio or Carnaroli
- 1 Tbsp extra-virgin olive oil
- 3 Tbsp unsalted butter
- 1 medium shallot, finely chopped
- 2 tsp finely chopped fresh sage
- 1 cup/240 ml Barolo wine
- 2 cups/480 ml chicken broth
- ½ cup/60 g freshly grated Parmigiano-Reggiano

TO MAKE THE CHICKEN: In a shallow dish, combine the olive oil, salt, and pepper. Put the porcini in another dish. Dip the chicken into the oil mixture and then coat with the porcini. Heat a large skillet over high heat and add the remaining oil mixture to the pan. Brown the chicken in batches (it will cook through in the rice cooker) and arrange in the steamer basket. Set aside.

TO MAKE THE RISOTTO: Place the rice in a sieve and rinse under a steady stream of cool water, stirring the grains. When the water runs clear, stop rinsing and shake the sieve to drain off excess water.

Set a medium rice cooker to the regular cycle or to quick cook if it's a fuzzy-logic machine. Heat the olive oil and 1 Tbsp of the butter until the butter melts. Add the shallot and sage and sauté for about 3 minutes or until the shallot begins to soften. Add the Barolo and bring to a boil. Stir in the rice and coat with the Barolo mixture. Add the chicken broth. Arrange the steamer basket over the rice cooker.

Cover the rice cooker and reset to the regular cycle or to the porridge cycle on a fuzzy-logic machine. Set a timer for 20 minutes. When the timer goes off, test the chicken for doneness (it should read 165°F/74°C on an instant-read thermometer). Slice the chicken into ½-in/12-mm strips. Stir the remaining 2 Tbsp butter and the Parmigiano into the risotto. Transfer the risotto to a serving platter, place the chicken over the risotto, and serve.

———

COOK'S NOTE: *If you have a difficult time finding a good aged Barolo, I would recommend a full-bodied red wine, such as Merlot, Barbera, Chianti, or Cabernet Sauvignon.*

TURKEY AND WILD RICE, RICE-COOKER STYLE

This dish is a takeoff on an old favorite at potluck dinners in the Midwest. It is the perfect vehicle for recycling leftover turkey from a holiday dinner. The wild rice turns creamy in the rice cooker and is studded with bits of celery, carrot, and dried cranberries.

WHAT YOU'LL NEED

- 1 cup/215 g wild rice
- 1 Tbsp unsalted butter
- 1 Tbsp extra-virgin olive oil
- ½ cup/80 g finely chopped red onion
- 2 celery ribs, finely chopped
- 1 medium carrot, peeled and finely chopped
- 1 tsp dried thyme
- 1½ cups/210 g cooked turkey or chicken, finely chopped

- ½ cup/85 g dried cranberries, chopped if large
- 2½ cups/600 ml chicken or vegetable broth
- Salt and freshly ground black pepper
- ¼ cup/25 g toasted sliced almonds
- 2 Tbsp finely chopped fresh flat-leaf parsley

Place the wild rice in a sieve and rinse under a steady stream of cool water, stirring the grains. When the water runs clear, stop rinsing and shake the sieve to drain off excess water.

Set a medium rice cooker to the regular cycle or to quick cook if it's a fuzzy-logic machine. Melt the butter with the olive oil. Add the onion, celery, carrot, and thyme and sauté for 3 minutes, or until the onion begins to soften. Add the rice, turkey, and cranberries, stirring to blend. Slowly stir in the chicken broth.

Cover the rice cooker and reset to the regular cycle. Set a timer for 25 minutes. When the timer goes off, check the rice; there should still be a bit of liquid in the pan. The rice should have split open, and it should be tender. Season with salt and pepper and transfer to a large serving bowl. Garnish with the almonds and chopped parsley before serving.

MEAT

PORK SHU MAI DUMPLINGS IN MISO SOUP

These savory dumplings flavored with soy, garlic, and ginger are given a bit of crunch from water chestnuts and green onions. They are steamed over a fragrant broth of miso enriched with greens for a great one-pot dinner on a hectic weeknight. Make the dumplings in the morning and steam everything together when you get home.

WHAT YOU'LL NEED

Dumplings

- 1 lb/455 g ground pork
- 2 Tbsp tamari or soy sauce
- 1 Tbsp toasted sesame oil
- 1 Tbsp mirin (Japanese sweet rice wine)
- 1 tsp grated peeled fresh ginger
- 2 garlic cloves, minced
- ½ cup/85 g finely chopped water chestnuts
- 2 green onions, white and tender green parts, finely chopped
- 1 Tbsp cornstarch
- One 10-oz/280-g package wonton wrappers

Soup

- 2 Tbsp vegetable oil
- 1 tsp grated peeled fresh ginger
- ½ cup/115 g white (shiro) miso
- 4 cups/960 ml chicken or vegetable broth
- 2 cups/280 g finely chopped greens, such as bok choy, Napa cabbage, or spinach
- 3 green onions; white and tender green parts, finely chopped; darker green parts, thinly sliced for garnish

TO MAKE THE DUMPLINGS: In a medium bowl, combine the pork, tamari, sesame oil, mirin, ginger, garlic, water chestnuts, green onions, and cornstarch, stirring until blended. Using a small portion scoop or a teaspoon, form the mixture into about twenty-four balls and place each one in the center of a wonton wrapper. Bring up the sides of the wrapper around the pork, twisting them closed to make a small purse out of the dough and sealing the edges with a bit of water. Set the finished dumplings on a baking sheet lined with parchment paper. (If you are not using them immediately, cover and refrigerate for up to 8 hours.)

TO MAKE THE SOUP: Set a medium rice cooker to the regular cycle or to quick cook if it's a fuzzy-logic machine. Heat the vegetable oil, add the ginger, and sauté for 1 minute, or until it is fragrant. Add the miso, chicken broth, and greens. Arrange the dumplings in two steamer baskets and place in the rice cooker.

Cover the rice cooker and reset to the regular cycle. Set a timer for 20 minutes. When the timer goes off, check to make sure the dumplings are cooked through (they should register 160°F/71°C on an instant-read thermometer). Remove the dumplings from the steamer baskets and place in a soup tureen. Add the green onions to the soup and pour over the dumplings. Serve immediately.

———

COOK'S NOTE: *To serve the shu mai as an appetizer, steam the dumplings over 4 cups/960 ml water in the rice cooker for 20 minutes. Meanwhile, in a small bowl, combine ¼ cup/60 ml tamari or soy sauce, 1 Tbsp rice vinegar, 2 tsp toasted sesame oil, 1 tsp chili-garlic sauce, ½ tsp grated peeled fresh ginger, and 2 tsp toasted sesame seeds. Serve right away. Any leftover dipping sauce will keep in the refrigerator for up to 2 days.*

PORK AND BROCCOLI STIR-FRY WITH NOODLES

For this savory dish, use the rice cooker to stir-fry the pork and vegetables and then steam the noodles in the basket. Use the ingredients list as your template, and change the protein and vegetables to suit your family's preferences. Use this dish as a vehicle for leftover vegetables such as broccoli, corn, or asparagus. If the vegetables are already cooked, stir them in when the noodles have finished cooking to warm them.

WHAT YOU'LL NEED

- 2 Tbsp vegetable oil
- 1 garlic clove, minced
- 1 tsp grated peeled fresh ginger
- ½ lb/225 g pork tenderloin, cut into ½-in/12-mm strips
- 1 medium onion, thinly sliced
- 1 cup/160 g broccoli florets
- ¼ cup/60 ml tamari or soy sauce
- 1 Tbsp ketchup
- 2 Tbsp rice vinegar

- ½ tsp chili-garlic sauce (optional)
- 2 tsp cornstarch
- ½ cup/120 ml chicken or vegetable broth
- 1 lb/455 g cooked fresh Asian-style thin wheat noodles (see Cook's Note, page 40) or cooked thin pasta strands
- 2 green onions, white and tender green parts, finely chopped
- ½ cup/55 g chopped roasted salted cashews

Set a medium rice cooker to the regular cycle or to quick cook if it's a fuzzy-logic machine. Heat the vegetable oil, add the garlic and ginger, and sauté for 30 seconds, or until fragrant. Add the pork and stir-fry until the pork is white on all sides (it may not be cooked through at this point). Remove the pork to a plate, add the onion and broccoli to the pan, and stir-fry until they begin to soften, about 3 minutes.

In a small bowl, stir together the tamari, ketchup, rice vinegar, chili-garlic sauce (if using), cornstarch, and chicken broth until the cornstarch is dissolved. Return the pork to the rice cooker and pour in the sauce, stirring to combine. Arrange the noodles in the steamer basket and set over the pork.

Cover the rice cooker and reset to the regular cycle. Set a timer for 10 minutes. When the timer goes off, transfer the noodles to a platter, stir the pork mixture, and arrange over the noodles. Sprinkle with the green onions and cashews and serve.

SAUSAGE AND PEPPERS WITH PARMESAN POLENTA

Simple to put together, this dish requires one pan to cook the peppers and sausage and your rice cooker to cook up some amazing polenta. You will love serving this not only during the week but also as a casual weekend dinner. Feel free to add a few spicy sausages to this if you prefer them to the sweet ones. The sweet peppers and tomato with a bit of aged balsamic vinegar pair well with the savory Parmesan polenta.

WHAT YOU'LL NEED

Sausage and Peppers

- 2 Tbsp extra-virgin olive oil
- 1½ lb/680 g sweet Italian sausage, or a mix of sweet and spicy
- 1 large sweet yellow onion, such as Vidalia, thinly sliced
- 1 large red bell pepper, cored, seeded, and thinly sliced
- 1 large yellow bell pepper, cored, seeded, and thinly sliced
- 1 large orange bell pepper, cored, seeded, and thinly sliced
- One 14½-oz/415-g can crushed tomatoes, with their juice
- ½ tsp dried oregano
- 2 Tbsp aged balsamic vinegar

- Salt and freshly ground black pepper
- ¼ cup/15 g finely chopped fresh basil
- ¼ cup/15 g finely chopped fresh flat-leaf parsley

Polenta

- 2 cups/480 ml water or vegetable or chicken broth
- 2 cups/480 ml whole milk
- 1 cup/140 g Italian coarse-grain polenta
- 1 tsp salt
- 3 Tbsp unsalted butter
- ½ cup/60 g freshly grated Parmigiano-Reggiano cheese

TO MAKE THE SAUSAGE AND PEPPERS: In a large skillet, heat the olive oil over medium-high heat. Sear the sausage, making sure that it is browned on all sides. Remove from the skillet and set aside. Add the onion and bell peppers to the skillet and sauté for 5 to 7 minutes, until the vegetables begin to soften. Add the tomatoes, oregano, and balsamic vinegar and bring to a boil. Return the sausages to the pan and simmer for 20 minutes, until the sauce is reduced and the sausages are cooked through. Taste for seasoning and adjust with salt and pepper. Stir in the basil and parsley and keep warm.

TO MAKE THE POLENTA: While the sausages are cooking, coat the inside of a medium rice cooker with nonstick cooking spray. Combine the water, milk, polenta, and salt in the rice cooker. Cover and set to the regular cycle. During the cycle, stir occasionally (adding more broth if it is evaporating too quickly). When the cooking cycle is complete, stir in the butter and Parmigiano.

Transfer the polenta to a platter and arrange the peppers and sausages over the polenta before serving.

————

COOK'S NOTE: *I have seen this dish served on a huge board, with the polenta spread over the board and the sausage and peppers covering the polenta. Everyone serves themselves from the board.*

SWEET SAUSAGE AND BROCCOLI RABE WITH FARRO

Flavored with nuggets of sweet Italian sausage and crisp broccoli rabe, this dish features chewy farro, an ancient Roman grain with a low gluten index and a lot of vitamins and nutrients. Feel free to substitute your favorite green for the broccoli rabe—Swiss chard, black kale, and broccolini are all good choices here.

WHAT YOU'LL NEED

- 1 cup/200 g pearled farro
- 2 Tbsp extra-virgin olive oil
- 2 garlic cloves, minced
- 1 bunch broccoli rabe, tough stems removed, finely chopped
- Salt and freshly ground black pepper
- ¾ lb/340 g bulk Italian sweet sausage

- ½ cup/80 g finely chopped red onion
- Grated zest of 1 lemon
- ⅔ cup/165 ml white wine (Sauvignon Blanc or Pinot Grigio)
- 1 cup/240 ml chicken or vegetable broth
- ½ cup/85 g golden raisins

Place the farro in a sieve and rinse under a steady stream of cool water, stirring the grains. When the water runs clear, stop rinsing and shake the sieve to drain off excess water.

Set a medium rice cooker to the regular cycle or to quick cook if it's a fuzzy-logic machine. Heat the olive oil, add the garlic, and sauté for 1 minute. Add the broccoli rabe and sauté for 3 minutes, or until softened. Remove the broccoli rabe from the rice cooker, season with salt and pepper, and set aside. Add the sausage to the rice cooker and sauté until it loses its pink color.

Remove all but 1 Tbsp of oil from the pan. Add the onion and lemon zest and sauté for another 3 minutes, or until the onion begins to soften. Add the farro, stirring up any bits on the bottom of the cooker. Add the wine and broth and stir to combine.

Cover the rice cooker and reset to the regular cycle. At the end of the cooking cycle, stir in the reserved broccoli rabe and any cooking liquid that has accumulated. Add the raisins, re-cover, and continue steaming for an additional 5 minutes on the keep-warm setting or with the machine turned off. (Many rice cookers, including all fuzzy-logic machines, do this automatically.) Serve warm.

BUTTERNUT SQUASH AND SAUSAGE RISOTTO WITH FRIED SAGE LEAVES

Risotto made with winter squash is typically enjoyed in Italy in the fall. This variation is one of my favorites, incorporating sweet sausage and sage leaves.

WHAT YOU'LL NEED

Fried Sage Leaves

- ¼ cup/60 ml extra-virgin olive oil
- 6 sage leaves

Risotto

- 1 cup/215 g medium-grain rice, such as Arborio or Carnaroli
- ½ lb/225 g sweet Italian sausage, removed from its casing

- 1 medium shallot, finely chopped
- 1½ cups/340 g finely chopped peeled and seeded butternut squash
- ¼ cup/60 ml white wine (Sauvignon Blanc or Pinot Grigio)
- 2½ cups/500 ml chicken or vegetable broth
- 2 Tbsp unsalted butter
- ⅓ cup/45 g freshly grated Parmigiano-Reggiano cheese

TO MAKE THE FRIED SAGE LEAVES: Set a medium rice cooker to the regular cycle or to quick cook if it's a fuzzy-logic machine. Heat the olive oil, add the sage leaves, and fry until they are crisp. Remove to paper towels and drain. Transfer the oil from the rice cooker to a measuring cup and set aside.

TO MAKE THE RISOTTO: Place the rice in a sieve and rinse under a steady stream of cool water, stirring the grains. When the water runs clear, stop rinsing and shake the sieve to drain off excess water.

Sauté the sausage in the rice cooker until it loses its pink color, breaking up any larger pieces. Add the shallot and butternut squash and cook for about 3 minutes, or until the shallot begins to soften. Add the wine and chicken broth and bring to a boil. Add the rice and stir to coat the grains.

Cover the rice cooker and reset to the regular cycle. At the end of the cooking cycle, check the risotto; there should still be a bit of liquid in the pan, and the rice should be al dente (still firm to the bite). Stir in the butter and half of the Parmigiano. Serve the risotto in shallow bowls, garnished with a drizzle of the sage oil and a leaf of sage, and pass the remaining Parmigiano on the side.

JAMBALAYA

In this classic Creole dish, nuggets of spicy andouille sausage are mixed with shrimp, rice, herbs, and spices, and the holy trinity of Louisiana Creole cooking—onion, celery, and bell pepper. It makes a great one-pot dinner for family or friends.

WHAT YOU'LL NEED

- 1½ cups/315 g long-grain rice
- ½ lb/225 g andouille or another smoked sausage
- 1 medium onion, finely chopped
- 2 celery ribs, finely chopped
- 1 medium red bell pepper, cored, seeded, and finely chopped
- 2 garlic cloves, minced
- ½ tsp sweet paprika
- ½ tsp dried thyme

- ¼ tsp dried oregano
- ⅛ tsp cayenne pepper
- 1 Tbsp tomato paste
- 2 cups/480 ml chicken or vegetable broth
- ½ lb/225 g large shrimp, peeled, deveined, and chopped
- 2 green onions, white and tender green parts, finely chopped
- Assorted hot sauces for serving

Place the rice in a sieve and rinse under a steady stream of cool water, stirring the grains. When the water runs clear, stop rinsing and shake the sieve to drain off excess water.

Set a medium rice cooker to the regular cycle or to quick cook if it's a fuzzy-logic machine. Sauté the sausage until it renders some fat. Add the onion, celery, bell pepper, garlic, paprika, thyme, oregano, and cayenne. Sauté for 3 to 4 minutes, or until the onion is translucent. Add the tomato paste and stir to blend. Stir in the rice and chicken broth.

Cover the rice cooker and reset to the regular cycle. At the end of the cooking cycle, stir in the shrimp and close the lid. Set a timer for 10 minutes. When the timer goes off, the shrimp should be pink and cooked through. Fluff the rice and garnish the jambalaya with the green onions. Pass the hot sauces on the side when serving.

PORTUGUESE SAUSAGE AND POACHED EGGS WITH SAFFRON TOMATO SAUCE

This hearty dish can be made for breakfast, lunch, or dinner. The tomato sauce is enriched with linguiça and fragrant with saffron and garlic. The eggs poach on the top of the sauce for about 5 minutes, for a soft yolk. If you like a firmer yolk, cook them for 7 minutes.

WHAT YOU'LL NEED

- ½ lb/225 g linguiça or another smoked sausage, cut into ½-in/12-mm rounds
- 1 large onion, finely chopped
- 1 garlic clove, minced
- 1 red bell pepper, cored, seeded, and finely chopped
- 1 tsp saffron threads, crushed in the palm of your hand
- One 14½- to 15-oz/415- to 430-g can chopped tomatoes, with their juice

- ½ cup/120 ml chicken broth
- Salt and freshly ground black pepper
- 4 large eggs
- 1 cup/100 g frozen petite peas, defrosted
- ¼ cup/15 g finely chopped fresh flat-leaf parsley
- Crusty bread for serving

Set a medium rice cooker to the regular cycle or to quick cook if it's a fuzzy-logic machine. Sauté the sausage, onion, and garlic for 3 minutes, or until the sausage has rendered some fat.

Remove all but 2 Tbsp of fat from the pan and add the bell pepper and saffron, stirring to coat the vegetables and meat with the saffron. Add the tomatoes and chicken broth and cover the rice cooker. Reset to the regular cycle and set a timer for 20 minutes. When the timer goes off, season the sauce with salt and pepper. Crack the eggs into a measuring cup. Add the peas to the sauce, slide the eggs over the sauce, and sprinkle with more salt and pepper, if desired.

Cover the rice cooker and cook for 5 minutes, until the eggs are set. (Depending on your rice cooker, this could take a bit longer.) Carefully remove the eggs from the rice cooker with some of the sauce, and plate them. Garnish with the chopped parsley and serve with crusty bread to mop up the delicious sauce.

OSSO BUCO MEATBALLS WITH TOMATO-PARMESAN RISOTTO

Osso buco is a traditional dish made with veal shanks that hails from the Emilia-Romagna region of Italy. In this adaptation, the flavors of osso buco—veal, wine, tomato, and saffron, plus a citrus and parsley garnish—take the form of meatballs. These are sautéed and then steamed over a delicious tomato and Parmesan risotto. The citrus-flecked meatballs and the rich aromas of the risotto will have your family waiting by the rice cooker for this dish to finish.

WHAT YOU'LL NEED

Meatballs

- 1 cup/55 g torn fresh bread
- 3 Tbsp milk
- 1 lb/455 g ground veal
- 1 tsp grated lemon zest
- 1 tsp grated orange zest
- 2 tsp minced flat-leaf parsley
- ⅛ tsp saffron threads, crushed in the palm of your hand
- 1 garlic clove, minced
- 1 large egg, beaten
- 1 cup/115 g dry bread crumbs
- Extra-virgin olive oil for frying

Risotto

- 2 cups/430 g medium-grain rice, such as Arborio or Carnaroli
- 4 Tbsp/55 g unsalted butter
- 1 Tbsp extra-virgin olive oil
- 1 medium shallot, finely chopped
- 2 fresh sage leaves, finely chopped
- 1½ cups/230 g cherry or pear tomatoes, chopped
- ¼ cup/60 ml dry white wine or dry vermouth
- 2¾ cups/660 ml chicken or vegetable broth
- ¼ cup/25 g chopped rinds from Parmigiano-Reggiano (optional), plus ⅓ cup/45 g freshly grated Parmigiano-Reggiano
- Basil for garnish (optional)

continued

TO MAKE THE MEATBALLS: Put the bread in a large mixing bowl and pour the milk over the bread. Let stand for 5 minutes, or until the milk is absorbed. Add the veal, lemon zest, orange zest, parsley, saffron, garlic, and egg and stir until the mixture is thoroughly combined. Spread out the dry bread crumbs in an even layer on a plate. Using a portion scoop, shape the mixture into 1-in/2.5-cm balls and then roll in the bread crumbs until coated. In a large skillet, heat ½ in/12 mm of olive oil and fry the meatballs in batches, turning frequently to give them a nice crust. Drain on paper towels. Arrange the meatballs in the steamer basket—you may have to stack them—and set aside. (At this point, you can cool the meatballs, refrigerate them for up to 8 hours, and then proceed with the recipe.)

TO MAKE THE RISOTTO: Place the rice in a sieve and rinse under a steady stream of cool water, stirring the grains. When the water runs clear, stop rinsing and shake the sieve to drain off excess water.

Set a medium rice cooker to the regular cycle or to quick cook if it's a fuzzy-logic machine. Melt the butter with the olive oil, add the shallot and sage, and sauté for 2 to 3 minutes, or until the shallot is translucent. Add the rice and tomatoes and sauté for another 3 minutes, until the tomatoes begin to soften. Add the wine, chicken broth, and Parmigiano rinds (if using). Arrange the steamer basket over the rice. Cover the rice cooker and reset to the regular cycle. Set a timer for 20 minutes. When the timer goes off, check the risotto; it should still have a bit of liquid in the pan, and the rice should be al dente (still firm to the bite). Remove the steamer basket, stir the grated Parmigiano into the risotto, and transfer to a platter. Arrange the meatballs on top of the risotto and garnish with basil (if using) before serving.

VEAL MEATBALLS OVER RICE
WITH BUTTERNUT SQUASH

This is a great dish to serve in the fall or winter—hearty veal meatballs over a bed of sweet-and-savory sage-scented rice with butternut squash.

WHAT
YOU'LL
NEED

Meatballs

- 1 cup/55 g torn fresh bread
- ¼ cup/60 ml milk
- 1 lb/455 g ground veal
- ½ large sweet yellow onion, such as Vidalia, finely chopped
- ¼ cup/15 g finely chopped fresh flat-leaf parsley
- 1½ tsp salt
- ½ tsp freshly ground black pepper
- 1 large egg, beaten
- Extra-virgin olive oil for frying

Rice

- 2 cups/430 g long-grain rice
- 2 Tbsp unsalted butter
- 1 Tbsp extra-virgin olive oil
- ½ large sweet yellow onion, such as Vidalia, finely chopped
- 2 tsp finely chopped fresh sage leaves
- 1½ cups/340 g peeled and finely diced butternut squash
- 3 cups/720 ml chicken or vegetable broth
- ½ cup/60 g freshly grated Parmigiano-Reggiano cheese

TO MAKE THE MEATBALLS: Put the bread into a large mixing bowl and pour the milk over the bread. Let stand for 5 minutes, or until the milk is absorbed. Add the veal, onion, parsley, salt, pepper, and egg and stir to thoroughly combine. Using a portion scoop, shape the mixture into 1-in/2.5-cm balls. In a large skillet, heat ½ in/12 mm of olive oil and brown the meatballs on all sides, in batches. Drain on paper towels. Arrange the meatballs in the steamer basket—you may have to stack them—and set aside. (At this point, you can cool the meatballs, refrigerate them for up to 8 hours, and then proceed with the recipe.)

TO MAKE THE RICE: Place the rice in a sieve and rinse under a steady stream of cool water, stirring the grains. When the water runs clear, stop rinsing and shake the sieve to drain off excess water.

Set a medium rice cooker to the regular cycle or to quick cook if it's a fuzzy-logic machine. Melt the butter with the olive oil; add the onion, sage, and butternut squash; and sauté for 3 to 4 minutes, or until the onion is softened. Add the rice and stir to combine. Gradually stir in the chicken broth. Arrange the steamer basket over the rice. Cover the rice cooker and reset to the regular cycle. At the end of the cooking cycle, remove the steamer basket, stir the Parmigiano into the rice, and transfer to a platter. Arrange the meatballs on top of the rice or around the outside of the platter to serve.

LAMB MEATBALLS WITH CHIMICHURRI RICE

Chimichurri, a sauce that is served in Argentina with grilled meats, gives this dish a lot of personality. Spicy lamb meatballs flavored with garlic and mint are browned, and then cooked over long-grain rice. At the end of the cooking time, the chimichurri is stirred into the rice, giving it a piquant flavor and gorgeous green color. The rice is delicious served with any grilled meat, if you prefer to serve it separately as a side dish.

WHAT YOU'LL NEED

Chimichurri

- 1½ cups/90 g packed fresh flat-leaf parsley
- 4 garlic cloves, minced
- Pinch of red pepper flakes
- 1 Tbsp finely chopped fresh oregano
- 2 Tbsp capers packed in brine, drained
- 2 Tbsp red wine vinegar
- 2 Tbsp extra-virgin olive oil

Meatballs

- 1 lb/455 g ground lamb
- 2 garlic cloves, minced
- Grated zest of 1 lemon
- 2 Tbsp finely chopped fresh mint
- ½ cup/80 g finely chopped red onion
- 1½ tsp salt
- ½ tsp freshly ground black pepper
- 1 large egg, beaten
- Extra-virgin olive oil for frying

Rice

- 2 cups/430 g long-grain rice
- 3 cups/720 ml chicken or vegetable broth

TO MAKE THE CHIMICHURRI: In a food processor or blender, process the parsley, garlic, red pepper flakes, oregano, capers, red wine vinegar, and olive oil until you have a smooth sauce. Set aside. (It will keep in the refrigerator for up to 4 days.)

TO MAKE THE MEATBALLS: In a large mixing bowl, stir together the lamb, garlic, lemon zest, mint, onion, salt, pepper, and egg until well combined. Using a portion scoop, shape the mixture into 1-in/2.5-cm balls. In a large skillet, heat ½ in/12 mm olive oil and brown the meatballs in batches. Drain on paper towels. Arrange the meatballs in a steamer basket—you may have to stack them—and set aside. (At this point, you can cool the meatballs, refrigerate them for up to 8 hours, and then proceed with the recipe.)

TO MAKE THE RICE: Place the rice in a sieve and rinse under a steady stream of cool water, stirring the grains. When the water runs clear, stop rinsing and shake the sieve to drain off excess water.

In a medium rice cooker, combine the rice and chicken broth, stirring until blended. Arrange the steamer basket over the rice.

Cover the rice cooker and set to the regular cycle. When the rice is done, remove the steamer basket. Add half of the chimichurri to the rice and stir to blend. Transfer the rice to a platter and arrange the meatballs over the rice, drizzling with a bit of the remaining chimichurri before serving.

SEEAFOOD

SEAFOOD

———

PAELLA

—

Okay, I know what you are thinking, "Paella in a rice cooker? She's gone over the edge." But it's possible to make paella in a rice cooker, especially if you don't want to make it for an army. This recipe is a template; you should feel free to substitute your favorite meats, seafood, and vegetables. The rice, aromatics, and liquid amounts are the standard; after that you can make it your own.

WHAT YOU'LL NEED

- 1 cup/215 g medium-grain rice, such as Carnaroli or Arborio
- 1 Tbsp extra-virgin olive oil
- 1 boneless, skinless chicken breast half (5 to 6 oz/140 to 170 g), finely chopped
- ½ cup/105 g finely chopped Spanish chorizo or sopressata (see Cook's Note)
- ½ cup/80 g finely chopped red onion
- 3 garlic cloves, minced
- 1 medium red bell pepper, cored, seeded, and finely chopped
- ¼ cup/60 ml dry white wine, such as Sauvignon Blanc or Pinot Grigio

- ½ tsp saffron threads, crushed in the palm of your hand
- One 14½-oz/415-g can chopped tomatoes, with their juice
- 2½ cups/600 ml chicken or vegetable broth
- 12 small clams in their shells, scrubbed
- ½ lb/225 g medium shrimp, peeled and deveined
- 1 cup/85 g shelled English peas, or frozen peas, defrosted
- 1 lemon, cut into wedges
- ¼ cup/15 g finely chopped fresh flat-leaf parsley

Place the rice in a sieve and rinse under a steady stream of cool water, stirring the grains. When the water runs clear, stop rinsing and shake the sieve to drain off excess water.

Set a medium rice cooker to the regular cycle or to quick cook if it's a fuzzy-logic machine. Heat the olive oil and sauté the chicken until it is white on all sides (it will cook through during the cooking cycle). Add the chorizo, onion, garlic, and bell pepper and sauté for 3 minutes, or until the onion begins to soften and the garlic is fragrant. Pour the wine into a small measuring cup and sprinkle the saffron over it. Add the tomatoes to the cooker, pour in the broth and wine, and bring to a boil. Stir in the rice.

continued

Cover the rice cooker and reset to the regular cycle. Set a timer for 20 minutes. When the timer goes off, there should still be liquid left in the pan. Arrange the clams in the steamer basket, with the hinges facing up. Stir the shrimp and peas into the rice. Place the steamer basket above the rice, close the lid, and set the timer for 5 minutes. When the timer goes off, check to make sure the clams have opened. If they haven't, close the lid, turn off the machine, and set the timer for another 5 minutes. At that point, discard any clams that haven't opened.

Remove the steamer basket and stir the rice. Transfer the rice to a large shallow bowl, arrange the clams around the bowl, and garnish with the lemon wedges. Sprinkle the paella with the parsley and serve.

———

COOK'S NOTE: *Spanish chorizo, which is like hard salami, can be a bit difficult to find. Sopressata is an Italian salami that makes an adequate substitute, or you can substitute your favorite smoked sausage.*

GARLICKY CLAM RISOTTO

Clams and garlic seem like a match made in culinary heaven, and this risotto will have your family clamoring for more. The garlic and fresh clams infuse the rice with their flavors and are finished with a kick of lemon and fresh parsley. If fresh clams aren't available, you can use canned clams and their juice.

WHAT YOU'LL NEED

- 1 cup/215 g medium-grain rice, such as Carnaroli or Arborio
- 3 Tbsp extra-virgin olive oil
- 6 garlic cloves, minced
- 1 cup/225 g shucked clams, coarsely chopped
- ½ cup/120 ml dry white wine, such as Sauvignon Blanc or Pinot Grigio
- 1 cup/240 ml chicken or vegetable broth
- 1½ cups/360 ml clam juice
- Grated zest of 1 lemon
- ¼ cup/15 g finely chopped fresh flat-leaf parsley
- Salt and freshly ground black pepper

Place the rice in a sieve and rinse under a steady stream of cool water, stirring the grains. When the water runs clear, stop rinsing and shake the sieve to drain off excess water.

Set a medium rice cooker to the regular cycle or to quick cook if it's a fuzzy-logic machine. Heat the olive oil, add the garlic and clams, and sauté for 1 minute. Add the rice and stir to coat with the oil mixture. Add the wine and bring to a boil. Gradually add the chicken broth and clam juice.

Cover the rice cooker and reset to the regular cycle. Set a timer for 20 minutes. When the timer goes off, check the risotto; the rice should be al dente (still firm to the bite). If it needs a bit more time, re-cover the cooker and let it sit for 5 minutes. Stir in the lemon zest and parsley and season with salt and pepper before serving.

COOK'S NOTE: *No self-respecting Italian would ever put cheese on a seafood pasta dish, and this one is so special, I don't advise it, either.*

BEER-STEAMED SHRIMP WITH LEMON FARRO

When peel-and-eat spicy shrimp are on the table, a fun time is had by all. Eating with hands instead of a fork seems to encourage conversation around the table; and everyone takes their time, since the spicy shrimp need to be washed down with copious amounts of cold beer! This dish makes a great dinner for two to four people. The shrimp steam over fragrant lemon-scented farro. You can substitute rice or another grain for the farro if you prefer.

WHAT YOU'LL NEED

- 2 lb/910 g large shrimp (see Cook's Note)
- 1 Tbsp Old Bay Seasoning
- Zest of 4 lemons, ⅔ cup/ 165 ml fresh lemon juice, plus lemon wedges for garnish
- One 12-oz/360-ml bottle beer
- 1 cup/200 g pearled farro
- 2 Tbsp extra-virgin olive oil

- 2 garlic cloves, minced
- 1⅓ cups/315 ml chicken or vegetable broth
- Salt and freshly ground black pepper
- ½ to 1 cup/115 to 225 g unsalted butter, melted
- An assortment of hot sauces for serving

In a large bowl, combine the shrimp, Old Bay, half the lemon zest, lemon juice, and beer. Cover and refrigerate at least 2 hours, or up to 8 hours.

Place the farro in a sieve and rinse under a steady stream of cool water, stirring the grains. When the water runs clear, stop rinsing and shake the sieve to drain off excess water.

Set a medium rice cooker to the regular cycle or to quick cook if it's a fuzzy-logic machine. Heat the olive oil, add the garlic and farro, and sauté for 1 minute to toast the farro. Slowly pour in the chicken broth.

Cover the rice cooker and reset to the regular cycle. Set a timer for 20 minutes. Meanwhile, drain the shrimp and arrange in the steamer basket; you may have to stack them. When the timer goes off, check the farro (add a bit more broth if necessary) and place the steamer basket over the farro.

continued

Cover the rice cooker and reset the timer for 10 minutes. When the timer goes off, the shrimp should be pink and cooked throughout, and the farro should be tender but still al dente (firm to the bite). Season the farro with salt and pepper, if needed. Stir in the remaining lemon zest. Transfer the farro to a large serving bowl, and put the shrimp in another bowl. Serve the shrimp with the melted butter for dipping, the lemon wedges, and the hot sauces. Make sure to have a good supply of napkins, empty bowls for shells, and hot towels to wipe sticky hands and faces.

———

COOK'S NOTE: *If you can find "easy peel" shrimp for this dish, I recommend them. They are slit down the back, making them easier to eat.*

CURRIED SHRIMP WITH BASMATI RICE

—

This spicy shrimp and rice dish makes a great entrée on a weekend. A bit of prep is needed, but then the rice cooker will take over and produce a beautiful dish, fragrant with coconut milk and curry.

WHAT YOU'LL NEED

- 1 cup/215 g basmati rice
- 2 Tbsp vegetable oil
- 2 garlic cloves, minced
- 2 tsp grated peeled fresh ginger
- 1 medium onion, finely chopped
- ½ tsp ground turmeric
- ½ tsp curry powder
- 1 tsp ground coriander
- One 14½-oz/415-g can chopped tomatoes, with their juice
- One 14-oz/420-ml can coconut milk
- 1½ lb/680 g medium shrimp, peeled and deveined
- ½ cup/30 g finely chopped fresh cilantro

Place the rice in a sieve and rinse under a steady stream of cool water, stirring the grains. When the water runs clear, stop rinsing and shake the sieve to drain off excess water.

Set a medium rice cooker to the regular cycle or to quick cook if it's a fuzzy-logic machine. Heat the vegetable oil; add the garlic, ginger, onion, turmeric, curry powder, and coriander; and sauté for 3 to 4 minutes, or until the onion is translucent and the spices are fragrant. Add the tomatoes, coconut milk, and rice, stirring to distribute the ingredients.

Cover the rice cooker and reset to the regular cycle. Set a timer for 20 minutes. When the timer goes off, add the shrimp, close the lid, and turn the machine off. Let the curry continue steaming for 5 minutes. Stir the curry and check to make sure that the shrimp have all turned pink and are cooked through. If they are not done, re-cover and allow the shrimp to sit for another 5 minutes. Stir in the cilantro and serve.

SWEET AND PUNGENT SHRIMP AND BROCCOLI WITH STEAMED RICE

One of my favorite dishes from Hong Kong is a sweet and pungent shrimp dish, redolent of ginger, spiked with a bit of hot red pepper, and coated with a sweet and spicy sauce. It lends itself well to steaming in a rice cooker. Bright green broccoli and red-glazed shrimp are a terrific combination for this weeknight meal. The shrimp need only a 10-minute soak in the marinade before cooking, so you can have this dish on the table in less than an hour.

WHAT YOU'LL NEED

- ¼ cup/50 g sugar
- ¼ cup/60 ml ketchup
- 1 Tbsp soy sauce
- 3 Tbsp rice vinegar
- 1 Tbsp mirin (Japanese sweet rice wine)
- 2 garlic cloves, minced
- 1 tsp grated peeled fresh ginger
- 1 tsp red pepper flakes

- 1½ lb/680 g large shrimp, peeled and deveined
- 1½ cups/315 g short-grain rice
- 1¾ cups/420 ml water
- 1 tsp salt
- 2 cups/320 g broccoli florets
- 2 green onions, white and tender green parts, finely chopped (optional)

In a small bowl, whisk together the sugar, ketchup, soy sauce, rice vinegar, mirin, garlic, ginger, and red pepper flakes. Add the shrimp and toss to coat. Cover and refrigerate for up to 2 hours.

Place the rice in a sieve and rinse under a steady stream of cool water, stirring the grains. When the water runs clear, stop rinsing and shake the sieve to drain off excess water.

Put the rice in a medium rice cooker. Cover with the 1¾ cups/420 ml water and add the salt. Cover and set to the regular cycle. Set a timer for 15 minutes. Meanwhile, arrange the broccoli in the steamer basket and top with the shrimp. When the timer goes off, arrange the steamer basket over the rice.

Re-cover the rice cooker and continue cooking until the end of the cycle (about 10 minutes more). When the rice is cooked, make sure the shrimp have cooked through and turned pink and the broccoli is tender. Allow the rice to continue steaming for an additional 10 minutes on the keep-warm setting or with the machine turned off. (Many rice cookers, including all fuzzy-logic machines, do this automatically.) Remove the steamer basket, fluff the rice, and mound the rice on a platter. Top with the shrimp and broccoli, and serve garnished with the chopped green onions, if desired, before serving.

SCAMPI WITH BROWN RICE PILAF

—

Nutty brown rice is the perfect bed for this garlicky oregano-and-lemon-scented shrimp dish. The shrimp steam above the brown rice and are drizzled with garlic butter at the end of the cooking time.

WHAT YOU'LL NEED

- 2 cups/430 g brown rice
- 4 Tbsp/60 ml extra-virgin olive oil
- ½ cup/80 g finely chopped sweet yellow onion, such as Vidalia
- Grated zest of 3 lemons
- 3½ cups/840 ml chicken or vegetable broth
- 1½ lb/680 g large shrimp, peeled and deveined

- ½ cup/115 g unsalted butter
- 6 garlic cloves, minced
- 1 Tbsp finely chopped fresh oregano
- ½ cup/120 ml dry white wine, such as Sauvignon Blanc or Pinot Grigio
- ¼ cup/15 g finely chopped fresh flat-leaf parsley

Place the rice in a sieve and rinse under a steady stream of cool water, stirring the grains. When the water runs clear, stop rinsing and shake the sieve to drain off excess water.

Set a medium rice cooker to the regular cycle or to quick cook if it's a fuzzy-logic machine. Heat 2 Tbsp of the olive oil and sauté the onion and two-thirds of the lemon zest for 1 minute, or until the lemon zest is fragrant. Add the rice and toast in the oil for 1 minute. Slowly add the chicken broth.

Cover the rice cooker and reset to the regular cycle. Set a timer for 20 minutes. Meanwhile, stack the shrimp in the steamer basket and set aside. In a small sauté pan, melt the butter with the remaining 2 Tbsp olive oil and sauté the garlic, oregano, and remaining lemon zest until the garlic is fragrant, about 2 minutes. Add the wine and bring to a boil. Add the parsley and remove the garlic butter from the heat.

When the timer goes off, arrange the steamer basket over the rice. Set the timer for 10 minutes. Rewarm the garlic butter. When the timer goes off again, the rice should be tender, and the shrimp should be pink and cooked through. Remove the steamer basket and transfer the rice to a platter. Arrange the shrimp over the rice and drizzle the garlic butter over the shrimp. Serve immediately.

NEW ORLEANS–STYLE BARBECUE SHRIMP WITH CHEESE AND BACON GRITS

Every restaurant in New Orleans has a rendition of this classic dish—sweet and spicy shrimp served over creamy grits. I've taken it one step further and added smoky bacon and sharp white cheddar to the grits, which are also delicious served with grilled meats or seafood.

WHAT YOU'LL NEED

Grits

- 1 cup/140 g coarse stone-ground grits
- 1¼ cups/300 ml chicken or vegetable broth
- 1½ cups/360 ml whole milk
- 1 tsp salt
- 4 strips bacon, cooked until crisp and crumbled
- 1½ cups/170 g finely shredded sharp white cheddar cheese
- 2 or 3 dashes Tabasco sauce (see Cook's Note)

Shrimp

- ½ cup/115 g unsalted butter
- 1 Tbsp extra-virgin olive oil
- 4 garlic cloves, minced
- 1 tsp dried oregano
- ½ tsp dried thyme
- ½ tsp sweet paprika
- ⅛ tsp freshly ground black pepper
- Pinch of cayenne pepper
- 2 Tbsp Worcestershire sauce
- ¼ cup/60 ml fresh lemon juice
- 1½ lb/680 g large shrimp, peeled and deveined
- ¼ cup/15 g chopped fresh flat-leaf parsley

TO MAKE THE GRITS: Coat the inside of a medium rice cooker with nonstick cooking spray. Add the grits, chicken broth, milk, and salt, stirring to combine. Cover and set to the regular cycle. During the cycle (which may take up to 30 minutes), stir the grits a few times. (If you need more liquid toward the end of the cooking time, stir in a little broth or milk.) When the grits are done, stir in the bacon, cheese, and Tabasco.

continued

TO MAKE THE SHRIMP: When the grits are about halfway through their cooking cycle, in a large skillet, melt the butter with the olive oil over medium heat and cook the garlic, stirring, until softened, about 3 minutes. Add the oregano, thyme, paprika, black pepper, and cayenne and cook for another 2 minutes, stirring so the spices don't burn. Add the Worcestershire and lemon juice and simmer for 1 minute. Add the shrimp and cook, stirring, until they turn completely pink, about 8 minutes.

Transfer the grits to a platter or individual bowls and top with the barbecue shrimp. Garnish with the parsley before serving.

———

COOK'S NOTE: *In place of ground black or white pepper to season the grits, Tabasco is a great substitute, adding a bit of spice as well as blending well with the cheese.*

MISO COD OVER BLACK RICE

—

More than a decade ago, chef Nobu Matsuhisa stunned the culinary world with his extraordinary miso-glazed black cod. Other chefs soon followed suit, glazing chicken, shrimp, and vegetables with this simple sweet-and-salty sauce. Black cod can be hard to find, so this recipe calls for ordinary cod, but other thick-fleshed fish like salmon, halibut, or swordfish taste extraordinary with this glaze. It's also good on grilled or steamed shrimp or chicken for a change of pace. Black rice has become the darling of the superfood craze, since it is high in antioxidants, protein, iron, and fiber. Called "forbidden rice" in ancient China, it was so rare that only the emperors ate it. If you can't find it, substitute brown rice or short-grain white rice.

WHAT YOU'LL NEED

- 1½ lb/680 g cod fillets, cut into 4 pieces
- ¼ cup/60 ml sake
- ¼ cup/60 ml white (shiro) miso
- 1 Tbsp sugar
- ½ cup/120 ml mirin (Japanese sweet rice wine)
- 2 cups/430 g black rice

- 3¾ cups/900 ml water
- 1 tsp salt
- 1 to 2 Tbsp toasted sesame oil
- 2 green onions, white and tender green parts, finely chopped
- 1 cup/170 g frozen shelled edamame, defrosted

Place the cod in a large zipper-top plastic bag. In a small mixing bowl, whisk together the sake, miso, sugar, and ¼ cup/60 ml of the mirin until blended. Pour over the cod in the bag, seal, and refrigerate for at least 2 hours, or up to 8 hours. When you are ready to start the rice, drain the marinade into a small saucepan and boil for 5 minutes. Keep warm while the rice is cooking. Arrange the cod in the steamer basket of the rice cooker and set aside.

Place the rice in a sieve and rinse under a steady stream of cool water, stirring the grains. When the water runs clear, stop rinsing and shake the sieve to drain off excess water.

Combine the rice, 3¾ cups/900 ml water, remaining ¼ cup/60 ml mirin, and the salt in a medium rice cooker. Cover and set to the regular cycle. Set a timer for 20 minutes. When the timer goes off, remove the lid and arrange the steamer basket over the rice. Re-cover the rice cooker and cook for another 10 minutes. Make sure the cod is cooked through (it should register 145°F/63°C on an instant-read thermometer). Fluff the rice and transfer to a large platter. Arrange the cod on top of the rice and drizzle with the warm marinade. Garnish with a drizzle of toasted sesame oil and sprinkle with the green onions and edamame before serving.

BAJA COD WITH GREEN RICE

Fish tacos are a staple here in San Diego. Fried or grilled fish is tucked into soft corn tortillas and topped with cabbage, cheese, and salsa. They are addictive, especially when served with a Mexican beer. In this riff on a fish taco, the fish steams over spicy, beer-infused rice. The Spicy Cabbage Slaw makes a great accompaniment.

WHAT YOU'LL NEED

- 1½ lb/680 g cod fillets
- 3 Tbsp extra-virgin olive oil
- ¼ cup/60 ml fresh lime juice, plus 1 Tbsp
- 2 Tbsp chopped fresh cilantro, plus ¼ cup/15 g finely chopped
- ½ tsp ground cumin

- 1½ cups/315 g long-grain white rice
- 2 cups/480 ml pale Mexican beer
- 3 green onions, white and tender green parts, finely chopped
- Spicy Cabbage Slaw (recipe follows) for serving (optional)

Place the cod fillets in a large zipper-top plastic bag. In a small bowl, whisk together 2 Tbsp of the olive oil, the ¼ cup/60 ml lime juice, 2 Tbsp cilantro, and cumin. Pour the mixture over the cod, seal the bag, and marinate in the refrigerator for at least 2 hours, or up to 6 hours.

Place the rice in a sieve and rinse under a steady stream of cool water, stirring the grains. When the water runs clear, stop rinsing and shake the sieve to drain off excess water.

Put the rice in a medium rice cooker and add the beer, remaining 1 Tbsp lime juice, and remaining 1 Tbsp olive oil, stirring to blend. Cover and set to the regular cycle. Set a timer for 20 minutes. When the timer goes off, drain the cod, discarding the marinade, and place the cod in the steamer basket over the rice. Continue with the cooking cycle. At the end of the cooking cycle, check the fish to make sure that it is cooked through (it should be opaque and register 145°F/63°C on an instant-read thermometer).

continued

Re-cover the rice cooker and allow the fish and rice to continue steaming for an additional 10 minutes on the keep-warm setting or with the machine turned off. (Many rice cookers, including all fuzzy-logic machines, do this automatically.) Remove the fish from the rice cooker. Fluff the rice and stir in the green onions and remaining ¼ cup/15 g cilantro. Mound the rice on a platter and place the fish on top. Serve the cabbage slaw on the side, if desired.

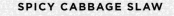

SPICY CABBAGE SLAW

SERVES 4 TO 6

Terrific to serve with fish tacos, this slaw makes a great contribution to a potluck. I love to serve it with Mexican food, but if you want to change it up a bit, sub in flat-leaf parsley for the cilantro for a Mediterranean flavor.

WHAT YOU'LL NEED

- 1 head green cabbage, cored and thinly sliced
- ½ cup/70 g thinly sliced red cabbage
- 1 medium carrot, peeled and coarsely grated
- ½ cup/120 ml rice vinegar
- ¼ cup/60 ml fresh orange juice
- ¾ cup/180 ml extra-virgin olive oil
- 1½ tsp salt
- ½ tsp freshly ground black pepper
- ⅛ tsp Tabasco or your favorite hot sauce
- ¼ cup/15 g finely chopped fresh cilantro

Put both cabbages and the carrot in a large mixing bowl. In a small mixing bowl, whisk together the rice vinegar, orange juice, olive oil, salt, pepper, and Tabasco. (Taste for seasoning and adjust if needed.) Pour the dressing over the vegetables and stir to blend. Add the cilantro and toss again. Serve immediately or cover and refrigerate for up to 8 hours.

COOK'S NOTE: *If you choose to make this ahead, drain off some of the water that collects in the bottom of the bowl before serving.*

HALIBUT WITH LEMON-DILL RICE

I always tell students who are afraid of serving fish to their families to start with halibut, since it reminds some people of chicken. Halibut is a thick-fleshed fish, with a firm texture and mild taste. It is delicious when steamed in your rice cooker. The lemon-dill rice will go well with any seafood or poultry dish.

WHAT YOU'LL NEED

- ¼ cup/60 ml extra-virgin olive oil
- 4 Tbsp/55 g unsalted butter, melted
- Grated zest of 2 lemons, plus 2 Tbsp fresh lemon juice
- 1½ lb/680 g halibut fillets
- 2 cups/430 g long-grain rice
- 3 cups/720 ml vegetable broth or water
- ¼ cup/15 g finely chopped fresh dill, plus more for garnish

In a large shallow bowl, combine the olive oil, butter, lemon zest, and lemon juice. Spoon out ¼ cup/ 60 ml of the lemony mixture into a small bowl and set aside. Put the halibut in the shallow bowl, turning the fish to coat with the remaining mixture, and set aside.

Place the rice in a sieve and rinse under a steady stream of cool water, stirring the grains. When the water runs clear, stop rinsing and shake the sieve to drain off excess water.

Combine the rice and vegetable broth in a medium rice cooker. Cover and set to the regular cycle. Set a timer for 10 minutes. When the timer goes off, arrange the halibut in the steamer basket over the rice. Re-cover the rice cooker and continue cooking until the cycle is complete. The halibut should be cooked through (it should register 145°F/63°C on an instant-read thermometer). Remove the fish from the rice cooker and cover with aluminum foil to keep warm. Stir the reserved lemon-butter mixture and the dill into the rice and cover. Allow the rice to continue steaming for an additional 5 minutes on the keep-warm setting or with the machine turned off. (Many rice cookers, including all fuzzy-logic machines, do this automatically.) Transfer the rice to a platter and place the fish on top. Garnish with more chopped dill and serve.

PARSLEY PESTO HALIBUT OVER WHITE RISOTTO

While testing this recipe, I found that basil pesto turned an unappetizing shade of olive green, but substituting parsley gave me a brilliant green color that complemented this lovely dish. White risotto is a plain risotto made with only a bit of onion and chicken broth and finished with butter and Parmigiano-Reggiano cheese. In Modena, Italy, they finish the risotto with a drizzle of traditionally made aged balsamic vinegar—mamma mia!

You will have plenty of pesto left over. See the Cook's Note for suggestions on what to do with it.

WHAT YOU'LL NEED

Pesto

- 1 cup/60 g packed fresh flat-leaf parsley leaves
- 1 cup/115 g walnuts
- 2 garlic cloves, peeled
- ½ cup/60 g freshly grated Parmigiano-Reggiano cheese
- 1 Tbsp capers in brine, drained
- ½ to ⅔ cup/120 to 165 ml extra-virgin olive oil

- 2 cups/430 g long-grain rice
- 4 Tbsp/55 g unsalted butter
- 1 Tbsp extra-virgin olive oil
- ½ cup/80 g finely chopped sweet onion, such as Vidalia
- ¼ cup/60 ml white wine or dry vermouth
- 2⅔ cups/630 ml chicken broth
- 1½ lb/680 g halibut fillets
- ⅓ cup/45 g freshly grated Parmigiano-Reggiano cheese

TO MAKE THE PESTO: In a food processor or blender, combine the parsley, walnuts, garlic, Parmigiano, and capers, pulsing to break up the nuts. With the machine running, add ½ cup/120 ml of the olive oil. This should be a paste, not a runny pesto. Add a little more oil if needed. Remove from the machine and pour into an airtight container, spooning 1 to 2 Tbsp olive oil over the top of the pesto to preserve its green color. You should have about 1½ to 2 cups/350 to 470 g. Set aside 1 cup/235 g for the halibut. Refrigerate the rest for up to 1 week or freeze for up to 3 months.

Place the rice in a sieve and rinse under a steady stream of cool water, stirring the grains. When the water runs clear, stop rinsing and shake the sieve to drain off excess water.

Set a medium rice cooker to the regular cycle or to quick cook if it's a fuzzy-logic machine, and melt 2 Tbsp of the butter with the olive oil. Sauté the onion for 3 minutes, or until it begins to soften. Add the wine, rice, and chicken broth.

Cover the rice cooker and reset to the regular cycle. Set a timer for 10 minutes. When the timer goes off, paint the halibut fillets with the pesto and arrange in a steamer basket. Place in the rice cooker and cover. Set the timer once more for 10 minutes. At the end of the cooking time, the halibut should be cooked through (it should register 145°F/63°C on an instant-read thermometer), and the rice should still have a bit of liquid in it.

Remove the halibut from the rice cooker and cover with aluminum foil to keep warm. Stir the remaining 2 Tbsp butter and the Parmigiano into the rice. Cover and allow to continue steaming for an additional 5 minutes on the keep-warm setting or with the machine turned off. (Many rice cookers, including all fuzzy-logic machines, do this automatically.) At this point the risotto should be al dente (firm to the bite), and there should still be a bit of liquid left in the pan. Transfer the risotto to a platter, place the halibut on top, and serve.

———

COOK'S NOTE: *The pesto is terrific on baguette slices. Or toss it into rice, pasta, pasta salad, or even potato salad. It's also delicious as a crust on broiled fish or chicken. Or add a bit more oil to it and use it as a sauce for grilled steak.*

MISO-GLAZED SEA BASS OVER QUINOA WITH VEGETABLES

Sweet miso flavors the sea bass, which steams over the vegetable-laden quinoa cooking below. The balance between the sweet meat of the fish and the savory quinoa is just right, and this easily assembled dish makes a great weeknight meal. If sea bass is not available, you can substitute cod, salmon, or halibut with delicious results.

WHAT YOU'LL NEED

- ¼ cup/50 g sugar
- ¼ cup/60 ml mirin (Japanese sweet rice wine)
- ¼ cup/55 g white (shiro) miso
- 2 Tbsp soy sauce
- Four 4- to 6-oz/115- to 170-g sea bass fillets (see Cook's Note)
- 1 Tbsp extra-virgin olive oil
- ¼ cup/40 g finely chopped red onion
- 1 medium zucchini, finely diced

- ½ cup/80 g finely chopped red bell pepper
- ½ cup/85 g corn kernels, cut fresh from the cob, or frozen kernels, defrosted
- 1½ cups/280 g prewashed quinoa
- 2¼ cups/540 ml chicken or vegetable broth
- Toasted sesame oil for garnish

In a small bowl, whisk together the sugar, mirin, miso, and soy sauce. Lay the fish on a plate and pour the marinade over it. Turn the fish to coat and refrigerate for at least 30 minutes, or up to 2 hours.

Set a medium rice cooker to the regular cycle or to quick cook if it's a fuzzy-logic machine. Heat the olive oil, add the red onion, and cook for 3 minutes, or until the onion is softened. Add the zucchini, bell pepper, and corn and toss with the oil. Add the quinoa and chicken broth and stir to combine. Drain the sea bass, discarding the marinade. Arrange the fish in a steamer basket and place over the quinoa.

Cover the rice cooker and reset to the regular cycle. At the end of the cooking cycle, fluff the quinoa and make sure the fish is cooked through (it should register 145°F/63°C on an instant-read thermometer). If it still needs some time, cover the machine and allow the residual heat to cook the fish. Transfer the quinoa to a platter and place the sea bass on top. Garnish with a drizzle of sesame oil and serve.

———

COOK'S NOTE: *Because of its protein structure, sea bass needs a bit more time than other thick-fleshed fish, so I begin cooking it when I cook the grain, and I leave it in the cooker until it's done. In other recipes for fish (such as salmon, cod, or halibut), you will note that the rice or other grain is given a bit of time to cook before the fish is added to the rice cooker.*

PARCHMENT-STEAMED SEA BASS VERACRUZ OVER CILANTRO QUINOA

The Mexican port of Veracruz is famous for its seafood. This dish is enjoyed in many iterations, made with either snapper or cod. But since the protein structure of sea bass will allow you to cook it in a rice cooker for the entire cooking cycle of the quinoa, it is the fish of choice here. Wrapped up in a packet of parchment paper along with Anaheim chile, tomatoes, and onion, the fish soaks up their flavors. It's a perfect dish to serve with quinoa. If you prefer to use rice or another grain, see the basic recipes in the first chapter and adapt one of them.

WHAT YOU'LL NEED

- 1½ lb/680 g sea bass fillets, cut into 4 portions
- 1½ cups/230 g cherry tomatoes, quartered
- 1 medium white onion, finely chopped
- 1 Anaheim chile, seeded, deribbed, and finely chopped
- ½ tsp ground cumin
- ¼ cup/60 ml extra-virgin olive oil
- 2 Tbsp fresh lime juice

- 1½ cups/280 g prewashed quinoa
- 2½ cups/600 ml chicken or vegetable broth
- ½ tsp salt
- ¼ tsp freshly ground black pepper
- ½ cup/30 g finely chopped fresh cilantro or flat-leaf parsley
- 1 Hass avocado, pitted, peeled, and thinly sliced (see Cook's Note)

Cut four pieces of parchment paper into 10-by-12-in/25-by-30.5-cm rectangles. Lay a piece of sea bass in the center of each piece of parchment. In a mixing bowl, stir together the tomatoes, onion, chile, cumin, olive oil, and lime juice. Top each piece of fish with some of the tomato-onion mixture. If you have extra, save it to garnish the quinoa. Fold the paper over the fish, and seal the edges by folding them over a few times to make a trim package. Stack the fish packages in the steamer basket of the rice cooker and set aside.

continued

Put the quinoa in a medium rice cooker and stir in the chicken broth, salt, and pepper. Arrange the steamer basket over the quinoa. Cover the rice cooker and set to the regular cycle. At the end of the cooking cycle, check the fish to make sure it is cooked through (it should register 145°F/63°C on an instant-read thermometer). Allow the fish and quinoa to continue steaming for an additional 5 minutes on the keep-warm setting or with the machine turned off. (Many rice cookers, including all fuzzy-logic machines, do this automatically.) Fluff the quinoa and stir in ¼ cup/15 g of the cilantro. Transfer the quinoa to a serving bowl. Open each packet of fish, lay a few slices of avocado over the fish, and sprinkle with the remaining cilantro. Plate the fish packets and serve.

———

COOK'S NOTE: *Want to keep that leftover avocado from turning brown? Spritz it with some water and then wrap it tightly in plastic wrap. I have even submerged the slices in water, and they have stayed beautifully green overnight.*

SOY-MARINATED SALMON WITH BOK CHOY AND COCONUT RICE

Salty and sweet is one of my favorite combinations, and this one-pot meal is a great example. The salmon is marinated in a soy-flavored sauce and then wrapped in bok choy leaves to steam over sweet and fragrant coconut rice. The marinade is cooked down to a syrupy glaze, which can be drizzled over the finished dish or used as a dipping sauce.

WHAT YOU'LL NEED

Salmon

- ½ cup/120 ml soy sauce
- ½ cup/120 ml water
- ½ cup/120 ml rice vinegar
- 2 Tbsp dark brown sugar
- 1 tsp chili-garlic sauce
- ¼ cup/15 g finely chopped fresh cilantro
- 2 tsp fresh lime juice

- 2 Tbsp seeded and finely chopped jalapeño chile
- Four ½-lb/225-g salmon fillets
- 1 head bok choy

Coconut Rice

- 1⅓ cups/280 g basmati rice
- 1 cup/240 ml coconut milk
- 1 cup/240 ml water

TO MAKE THE SALMON: In a small mixing bowl, whisk together the soy sauce, water, rice vinegar, brown sugar, chili-garlic sauce, cilantro, lime juice, and jalapeño. Put the salmon into a large zipper-top plastic bag and pour the marinade over the salmon. Seal the bag and refrigerate for at least 2 hours, and up to 6 hours.

Cut off the root end of the bok choy and separate the leaves. Place on a microwavable plate and cover with damp paper towels. Microwave on high until the bok choy is pliable, about 1½ minutes. Set aside to cool.

continued

Remove the salmon from the marinade and pour the marinade into a small saucepan. Bring to a boil and continue boiling for 5 minutes. Lower the heat and simmer until the marinade has a syrupy consistency, about 15 minutes more. Wrap each piece of salmon in a leaf of bok choy, securing it with a toothpick or a silicone band. Chop the remaining bok choy into ½-in/12-mm ribbons and line the steamer basket with the chopped bok choy. Stack the salmon packets on top and set aside.

TO MAKE THE COCONUT RICE: Place the rice in a sieve and rinse under a steady stream of cool water, stirring the grains. When the water runs clear, stop rinsing and shake the sieve to drain off excess water.

Put the rice in a medium rice cooker and stir in the coconut milk and 1 cup/240 ml water. Cover and set to the regular cycle. Set a timer for 10 minutes. When the timer goes off, put the steamer basket over the rice, cover, and continue cooking. At the end of the cooking cycle, check to make sure the salmon is cooked through (it should be opaque and register 145°F/63°C on an instant-read thermometer).

Re-cover the rice cooker and allow the rice and salmon to continue steaming for an additional 10 minutes on the keep-warm setting or with the machine turned off. (Many rice cookers, including all fuzzy-logic machines, do this automatically.) Meanwhile, rewarm the marinade, which is now a sauce. Mound the rice on a platter, remove the toothpicks or silicone bands from the salmon packets, and arrange the salmon on top of the rice. Distribute the chopped bok choy around the edges of the platter and drizzle a bit of the sauce over the bok choy and the salmon packets. Serve the remaining sauce warm on the side.

CAJUN SALMON WITH DIRTY RICE AND FRUIT SALSA

Salmon rubbed with Cajun seasonings, and then cooked over a potful of New Orleans–style spicy "dirty rice," makes a terrific meal any night of the week. Serve the fruit salsa alongside the salmon to cool the heat a bit. Note that the salsa needs to chill for a couple of hours before you serve it.

WHAT YOU'LL NEED

- 2 cups/430 g long-grain rice
- ¼ cup/60 ml extra-virgin olive oil
- 2 Tbsp Cajun Seasoning, homemade (recipe follows) or store bought
- 1½ lb/675 g salmon fillets
- ½ lb/225 g pork breakfast sausages, removed from their casings
- 1 medium onion, finely chopped
- 2 celery ribs, finely chopped
- ¼ cup/40 g finely chopped green bell pepper
- 2 garlic cloves, minced
- Pinch of cayenne pepper
- 2 tsp dried thyme leaves
- 3 cups/720 ml chicken broth
- Fruit Salsa (page 127) for serving

Place the rice in a sieve and rinse under a steady stream of cool water, stirring the grains. When the water runs clear, stop rinsing and shake the sieve to drain off excess water.

In a small bowl, combine the olive oil and Cajun seasoning. Paint the salmon on both sides with the oil mixture and set aside.

Set a medium rice cooker to the regular cycle or to quick cook if it's a fuzzy-logic machine. Cook the sausage until it is no longer pink. Discard all but 1 Tbsp of the fat in the rice cooker. Add the onion, celery, bell pepper, garlic, cayenne, and thyme and sauté for 2 to 3 minutes; the vegetables will be fragrant. Add the rice and chicken broth. Reset the rice cooker to the regular cycle and set a timer for 10 minutes. When the timer goes off, arrange the salmon in the steamer basket, and place over the rice.

continued

Cover the rice cooker and continue with the cooking cycle. At the end of the cooking cycle, check the salmon to make sure it is cooked through (it should register 145°F/63°C on an instant-read thermometer). Remove the fish from the rice cooker and allow the rice to continue steaming for an additional 5 minutes on the keep-warm setting or with the machine turned off. (Many rice cookers, including all fuzzy-logic machines, do this automatically.) Transfer the rice to a large platter and place the salmon on top. Put the fruit salsa in a decorative bowl and serve it alongside the fish and rice.

CAJUN SEASONING

MAKES ½ CUP/70 G

Cajun seasoning is a zesty mix of herbs and spices that enhances seafood, chicken, and pork. Use it as a rub for grilling, to season rice or grains, and to sprinkle on popcorn or oven fries. If you would like to tone down the heat a bit, halve the amount of cayenne pepper.

WHAT YOU'LL NEED

- 3 Tbsp sea salt
- 1 Tbsp sweet paprika
- 1 Tbsp onion powder
- 1 Tbsp garlic powder
- 1 tsp cayenne pepper

- ½ tsp ground white pepper
- ½ tsp freshly ground black pepper
- 2 tsp dried thyme leaves
- 1 tsp dried oregano leaves

In a large bowl, combine the sea salt, paprika, onion powder, garlic powder, cayenne, white pepper, black pepper, thyme, and oregano. Transfer to an airtight container. Store in a cool, dry place for up to 6 months.

MAKES 2 CUPS/360 G

Fruit salsas are terrific accompaniments for seafood, poultry, or pork. I like to use fresh fruits that are in season; the basic formula will work with whatever fruit you have on hand. If you like, combine several fruits for a multicolored salsa. And feel free to add or subtract other ingredients to suit your taste. Don't care for raw onion? Just omit it.

WHAT YOU'LL NEED

- 1½ cups/240 g finely diced peeled fresh fruit (see Cook's Note)
- ½ cup/80 g finely diced red onion
- ½ cup/80 g finely chopped red or yellow bell pepper
- 1 tsp finely diced jalapeño chile
- 2 Tbsp finely chopped fresh cilantro or flat-leaf parsley

- 2 Tbsp fresh lemon, orange, or lime juice, or rice vinegar
- 2 Tbsp extra-virgin olive oil
- ½ tsp salt
- 3 or 4 dashes hot sauce (optional)

Stir the fruit, red onion, bell pepper, jalapeño, cilantro, lemon juice, olive oil, salt, and hot sauce (if using) together in a medium mixing bowl. Cover and refrigerate for at least 2 hours, or up to 3 days.

COOK'S NOTE: *Fruit salsas are a great way to use up leftover fruit. Good choices are a combination of stone fruits, such as peaches, nectarines, and apricots; citrus fruits, such as orange, tangerine, and grapefruit; or tropical fruits, such as mango, pineapple, and papaya.*

VEGETABLES AND GRAINS

FARRO
MINESTRONE

Il Panaro, a small restaurant and bar outside Gubbio, my grandparents' hometown, serves a version of this soup that I dream about. The basic minestrone is enhanced by chewy farro, some of which is puréed to thicken the soup, while the rest is left whole. Unlike some of its counterparts, this minestrone has no tomato in it.

WHAT YOU'LL NEED

- 1 cup/200 g pearled farro
- 2 Tbsp extra-virgin olive oil, plus more for drizzling
- 1 medium onion, finely chopped
- 2 celery ribs, with their leaves, finely chopped
- 2 medium carrots, peeled and finely chopped
- 4 cups/960 ml chicken or vegetable broth
- ¼ cup/15 g finely chopped fresh flat-leaf parsley
- Salt and freshly ground black pepper

Place the farro in a sieve and rinse under a steady stream of cool water, stirring the grains. When the water runs clear, stop rinsing and shake the sieve to drain off excess water.

Set a medium rice cooker to the regular cycle or to quick cook if it's a fuzzy-logic machine. Heat the olive oil; add the onion, celery, and carrots; and sauté for 3 to 4 minutes, or until the onion begins to soften. Add the farro and chicken broth.

Cover the rice cooker and reset to the regular cycle. Set a timer for 20 minutes. When the timer goes off, check to see if the farro has become tender. If it's not quite done, let sit, covered, on the keep-warm setting or with the machine turned off. Using a soup ladle, remove a ladleful of the farro and vegetables to a bowl. Purée the rest of the soup with an immersion blender. (If you don't have one, cool the soup slightly and use a blender or food processor.) Return the reserved farro and vegetables to the soup. Add the parsley and season with salt and pepper. Drizzle each bowl of soup with olive oil before serving.

ITALIAN CHICKPEA AND PASTA SOUP

This simple peasant soup from the hills of Calabria is a great warmer on a cold day. It's fragrant with garlic, rosemary, and tomatoes and packed with chickpeas and tiny ditali for a hearty and satisfying dish.

WHAT YOU'LL NEED

- 1 Tbsp extra-virgin olive oil
- 2 garlic cloves, minced
- 1 medium onion, finely chopped
- 2 tsp finely chopped fresh rosemary
- One 14½-oz/415-g can chopped tomatoes, with their juice
- Salt and freshly ground black pepper
- 3 cups/720 ml chicken or vegetable broth

- Two 14½-oz/415-g cans chickpeas, rinsed and drained
- ½ cup/50 g ditali or another small pasta
- ¼ cup/15 g finely chopped fresh flat-leaf parsley
- Freshly grated Pecorino Romano cheese for garnish

Set a medium rice cooker to the regular cycle or to quick cook if it's a fuzzy-logic machine. Warm the olive oil; add the garlic, onion, and rosemary; and sauté for 2 to 3 minutes, or until the vegetables are translucent. Add the tomatoes and sauté for another 2 minutes. Add 1 tsp salt, ½ tsp pepper, the chicken broth, chickpeas, and ditali.

Cover the rice cooker and reset to the regular cycle. Set a timer for 30 minutes. When the timer goes off, stir in the parsley and season with salt and pepper if needed. Serve the soup in deep bowls, garnished with grated Pecorino Romano cheese.

NONNA'S VEGETABLE SOUP

Many people associate humble Italian vegetable soup with Tuscany or Umbria, but in fact, there are variations on minestrone served all over Italy. This is the one my Nonna Aleandra used to make. She would vary the ingredients with the season, but its components were vegetables, water, some legumes, and possibly some leftover pasta thrown in at the end. Humble cucina povera, *or "food of the poor," it's a delicious warmer on a cold fall or winter day.*

WHAT YOU'LL NEED

- 2 Tbsp extra-virgin olive oil
- ½ cup/80 g finely chopped sweet yellow onion, such as Vidalia
- 2 celery ribs, finely chopped
- 1 medium carrot, peeled and finely chopped
- 1 tsp dried sage leaves
- 1 cup/155 g canned crushed tomatoes, with their juice
- 4 cups/960 ml chicken or vegetable broth
- 1 medium zucchini, coarsely chopped

- ¼ lb/115 g green beans, trimmed and cut into 1-in/2.5-cm pieces
- 1 cup/140 g finely chopped savoy cabbage, spinach, or black kale
- ⅓ cup/65 g lentils
- Rind from Parmigiano-Reggiano cheese (about 1 in/2.5 cm square), cut into small dice (optional), plus ⅓ cup/45 g finely shredded Parmigiano-Reggiano cheese
- Salt and freshly ground black pepper

Set a medium rice cooker to the regular cycle or to quick cook if it's a fuzzy-logic machine. Heat the olive oil; add the onion, celery, carrot, and sage leaves; and sauté for 3 minutes, or until the vegetables begin to soften. Add the tomatoes, chicken broth, zucchini, green beans, cabbage, lentils, and Parmigiano rind (if using).

Cover the rice cooker and set to the regular cycle. Set a timer for 30 minutes. When the timer goes off, check the soup, and make sure the lentils are cooked. They should have split open and thickened the soup. Season with salt and pepper if needed. Keep the soup warm until ready to serve. (If you would like a thinner soup, add a bit more broth or water, adjusting the seasonings accordingly.) Garnish each bowl of soup with shredded Parmigiano and serve.

TOMATO-PARMESAN SOUP WITH RICOTTA AND SPINACH DUMPLINGS

The combination of the robust tomato and Parmesan soup and the delicate dumplings is comfort food to soothe the soul—and it all happens in your rice cooker! You will need the rind from Parmigiano-Reggiano cheese to flavor this soup.

WHAT YOU'LL NEED

Soup

- 2 Tbsp extra-virgin olive oil
- 2 garlic cloves, minced
- 1 medium onion, finely chopped
- 2 medium carrots, peeled and finely chopped
- One 14½-oz/415-g can crushed tomatoes, with their juices
- 2½ cups/600 ml chicken or vegetable broth
- Rind from Parmigiano-Reggiano cheese (about 1 in/2.5 cm square), coarsely chopped

Dumplings

- 2 cups/280 g frozen chopped spinach, defrosted and thoroughly drained
- ¾ cup/185 g whole-milk ricotta cheese
- ½ cup/60 g freshly grated Parmigiano-Reggiano cheese
- 1 cup/55 g fresh bread crumbs
- 1 large egg, lightly beaten
- ⅛ tsp freshly grated nutmeg
- 1 tsp salt
- ½ tsp freshly ground black pepper

- ½ cup/60 g freshly shredded Parmigiano-Reggiano cheese
- ¼ cup/15 g thinly sliced fresh basil

continued

TO MAKE THE SOUP: Set a medium rice cooker to the regular cycle or to quick cook if it's a fuzzy-logic machine. Heat the olive oil; add the garlic, onion, and carrots; and sauté until the onion is softened, 2 to 3 minutes. Add the tomatoes, chicken broth, and Parmigiano rind. Cover the rice cooker and reset to the regular cycle. Set a timer for 30 minutes.

TO MAKE THE DUMPLINGS: In a large bowl, combine the spinach, ricotta, grated Parmigiano, bread crumbs, egg, nutmeg, salt, and pepper, stirring until well blended. Using a portion scoop, shape the dough into balls about 1 in/2.5 cm in diameter.

When the timer goes off, carefully add the dumplings to the soup. Cover and cook for an additional 10 minutes. Garnish each bowl of soup with some of the shredded Parmigiano-Reggiano and basil, and serve.

TUSCAN WHITE BEAN SOUP WITH ROSEMARY AND PANCETTA

Here is a lovely way to combine some classic flavors from Umbria and Tuscany. The salty pancetta flavors the beans, giving you a delicious and hearty winter soup. Make sure to soak the beans for 8 hours before proceeding with the recipe or use the quick-soak method (see page 33). Mangia bene!

WHAT YOU'LL NEED

- 2 Tbsp extra-virgin olive oil, plus more for drizzling
- One ½-in-/12-mm-thick slice pancetta, finely diced
- 2 garlic cloves, minced
- 1 medium onion, finely chopped
- 2 Tbsp chopped fresh rosemary
- 2 medium carrots, peeled and coarsely chopped

- 2 celery ribs, coarsely chopped
- 1 cup/200 g small dried white beans, such as navy beans, soaked in cold water for 8 hours, rinsed, and drained
- 4 cups/960 ml chicken or vegetable broth, plus more if needed
- Salt and freshly ground black pepper

Set a medium rice cooker to the regular cycle or to quick cook if it's a fuzzy-logic machine. Heat the olive oil, add the pancetta, and cook until crispy. Add the garlic, onion, and rosemary and sauté for 2 to 3 minutes to soften the onion. Add the carrots, celery, and beans and stir to combine. Slowly add the chicken broth.

Cover the rice cooker and reset to the regular cycle. Set a timer for 1 hour. Check the beans from time to time to make sure that they are not sticking to the bottom of the pan. At the end of the hour, taste the beans to make sure they are soft and creamy; if not, set the timer for an additional 15 minutes. When the timer goes off, season the soup with salt and pepper if needed. Serve the soup with a drizzle of extra-virgin olive oil.

COOK'S NOTE: *If you would prefer to make this dish vegetarian, omit the pancetta and add an extra 1 Tbsp olive oil to the rice cooker.*

MEDITERRANEAN VEGETABLE AND BULGUR STEW

A lovely one-pot meal, this earthy vegetable stew will remind you of ratatouille, but with the added protein of bulgur. I like to serve this with a sprinkle of Gruyère and Parmesan over the top.

WHAT YOU'LL NEED

- ½ cup/105 g bulgur
- 2 Tbsp extra-virgin olive oil
- 2 garlic cloves, minced
- Pinch of red pepper flakes
- 1 medium red onion, finely chopped
- 1½ tsp herbes de Provence
- 2 Japanese eggplants, trimmed and finely chopped
- ½ cup/80 g coarsely chopped red bell pepper
- 2 small zucchini, trimmed and coarsely chopped

- One 14½-oz/415-g can chopped tomatoes, with their juice
- 2 cups/480 ml chicken or vegetable broth
- Salt and freshly ground black pepper
- ¼ cup/15 g finely chopped fresh flat-leaf parsley
- ½ cup/60 g freshly grated Parmigiano-Reggiano cheese
- ¼ cup/30 g finely shredded Gruyère or imported Swiss cheese

Place the bulgur in a sieve and rinse under a steady stream of cool water, stirring the grains. When the water runs clear, stop rinsing and shake the sieve to drain off excess water.

Set a medium rice cooker to the regular cycle or to quick cook if it's a fuzzy-logic machine. Heat the olive oil, add the garlic and red pepper flakes, and sauté for 30 seconds, or until fragrant. Add the onion and herbes de Provence and sauté for 2 to 3 minutes, until the onion begins to soften. Add the eggplants, bell pepper, and zucchini and sauté another 3 minutes to soften the vegetables. Add the tomatoes and bulgur and stir to combine. Slowly add the chicken broth.

Cover the rice cooker and reset to the regular cycle. At the end of the cooking cycle, season the stew with salt and pepper if necessary. Stir in the parsley and serve the stew, garnished with the cheeses.

UMBRIAN LENTIL STEW WITH FARRO

A thick, souplike preparation, this good-for-you dish from the green heart of Italy is flavored with lots of celery and thickened with the lentils and farro for a hearty dish to serve during the fall or winter.

WHAT YOU'LL NEED

- ½ cup/100 g pearled farro
- 2 Tbsp extra-virgin olive oil
- 1 bunch celery with the leaves, tough outer stalks removed, coarsely chopped
- 1 tsp dried sage leaves, crumbled in the palm of your hand

- ½ cup/100 g brown lentils, preferably small Italian ones
- 4 cups/960 ml chicken or vegetable broth, plus more if needed (see Cook's Note)
- Salt and freshly ground black pepper

Place the farro in a sieve and rinse under a steady stream of cool water, stirring the grains. When the water runs clear, stop rinsing and shake the sieve to drain off excess water.

Set a medium rice cooker to the regular cycle or to quick cook if it's a fuzzy-logic machine. Heat the olive oil and sauté the celery and sage for 2 to 3 minutes, or until the celery is coated with the oil and begins to soften. Add the farro and lentils and stir to combine. Slowly add the chicken broth.

Cover the rice cooker and reset to the regular cycle. Set a timer for 20 minutes. When the timer goes off, make sure the stew has enough liquid and add more broth if needed. Continue cooking for 20 minutes more; the stew should be thick but still have some liquid in the cooker. Season the stew with salt and pepper, if needed, and serve.

COOK'S NOTE: *Some lentils and farro will absorb liquid faster than others, so make sure to have more broth on hand to add if necessary.*

BLACK KALE AND FARRO WITH GARLIC–PINE NUT PESTO

Black kale is also known as lacinato kale, dinosaur kale, and, in Italy, cavolo nero. Whatever you choose to call the dark leafy green, it is really good for you. This dish also contains nutty farro and a crunchy, garlicky pesto, which makes it scrumptious as well as healthful. The pesto is delicious tossed with pasta.

WHAT YOU'LL NEED

Pesto

- 1 cup/120 g freshly grated Parmigiano-Reggiano cheese
- ½ cup/55 g pine nuts
- Pinch of red pepper flakes
- 6 garlic cloves, peeled
- ½ cup/120 ml extra-virgin olive oil

- 1 cup/200 g pearled farro
- 2 Tbsp extra-virgin olive oil
- 1 bunch black kale, tough stems trimmed, leaves cut into thin ribbons
- 1⅔ cups/405 ml chicken or vegetable broth
- 1 tsp salt
- ½ tsp freshly ground black pepper

TO MAKE THE PESTO: In a blender or food processor, combine the Parmigiano, pine nuts, red pepper flakes, and garlic. Pulse on and off to break up the nuts and garlic. With the machine running, slowly add the olive oil and process until the mixture comes together. Store in the refrigerator for up to 5 days.

Place the farro in a sieve and rinse under a steady stream of cool water, stirring the grains. When the water runs clear, stop rinsing and shake the sieve to drain off excess water.

Set a medium rice cooker to the regular cycle or to quick cook if it's a fuzzy-logic machine. Heat the olive oil, add the kale (it will look like it wants to jump out of the pan), and cover the rice cooker. Allow the kale to steam for 2 minutes and turn with tongs to coat in the oil. When the kale is wilted, add the farro and toss to coat the grains. Add the chicken broth, salt, and pepper.

Cover the rice cooker and set to the regular cycle. At the end of the cooking cycle, stir the farro and add ½ cup/115 g of the pesto, stirring to blend. Taste for seasoning and add more pesto if desired. Serve warm.

GREEK SALAD WITH GRAINS AND LEMON-DILL VINAIGRETTE

—

Studded with tomatoes, cucumbers, olives, and feta cheese, this salad is terrific made with long-grain white rice, wild rice, brown rice, barley, or bulgur. The lemon-dill dressing gives it a lovely finish. If you would like to add protein to the salad, cooked seafood, poultry, and lamb are all great add-ins.

WHAT YOU'LL NEED

- 3 cups/495 to 690 g freshly cooked grain of your choice (see Cook's Note)
- ½ cup/120 ml extra-virgin olive oil
- Grated zest of 1 lemon, plus ¼ cup/60 ml fresh lemon juice
- 1 garlic clove, minced
- 1 Tbsp plus 1 tsp finely chopped fresh dill, or 2 tsp dried
- Salt and freshly ground black pepper

- 1 cup/230 g finely diced unpeeled European or Asian cucumber
- 1 cup/155 g cherry tomatoes, halved, or quartered if large
- ½ cup/85 g pitted Kalamata olives, coarsely chopped
- ½ cup/110 g crumbled feta cheese
- ¼ cup/30 g finely chopped fresh flat-leaf parsley

Put the warm grain in a large serving bowl. In a small bowl, whisk together the olive oil, red wine lemon zest, lemon juice, garlic, and dill. Season with salt and pepper if needed. Toss the grain with some of the dressing, and reserve the rest for finishing.

When the grain has cooled, add the cucumber, tomatoes, olives, feta, and parsley to the bowl and toss to combine. Add more dressing if needed. Refrigerate the salad and any leftover dressing for up to 12 hours. Remove the salad from the refrigerator 30 minutes before serving and toss with additional dressing, if needed.

—

COOK'S NOTE: *The weight of the cooked grain depends on the type of grain. For this recipe, you'll need 495 g of cooked farro, 585 g of cooked rice, or 690 g of cooked wild rice, quinoa, or bulgur.*

GRAIN SALAD WITH ARTICHOKES, TOMATOES, AND FRESH MOZZARELLA

I love making this salad with farro, an ancient Roman grain, but brown rice, barley, wild rice, and brown basmati are all winners here. Tender artichoke hearts, along with tomatoes and tiny chunks of fresh mozzarella cheese, add zest and visual appeal to this scrumptious salad.

WHAT YOU'LL NEED

- 3 cups/495 to 690 g freshly cooked grain of your choice (see Cook's Note, page 143)
- ½ cup/120 ml extra-virgin olive oil
- 3 Tbsp red wine vinegar
- 1 garlic clove, minced
- ½ tsp sugar
- 1 tsp salt
- ½ tsp freshly ground black pepper
- ¼ cup/20 g packed fresh basil leaves, finely chopped

- One 10-oz/280-g package frozen artichoke hearts, defrosted, drained, and coarsely chopped
- 1 cup/155 g cherry or pear tomatoes, halved, or quartered if large
- 2 green onions, white and tender green parts, finely chopped
- ½ lb/225 g fresh mozzarella, cut into ½-in/12-mm dice

Put the warm grain in a large serving bowl. In a small bowl, whisk together the olive oil, red wine vinegar, garlic, sugar, salt, and pepper. Toss the grain with some of the dressing, and reserve the rest for finishing.

When the grain has cooled, add the basil, artichoke hearts, tomatoes, green onions, and mozzarella to the bowl and toss to combine. Add more dressing if needed. Refrigerate the salad and any leftover dressing for up to 12 hours. Remove the salad from the refrigerator 30 minutes before serving and toss with additional dressing, if needed.

SUMMERTIME GRAIN SALAD WITH TOMATOES, ZUCCHINI, AND BASIL

___

I love this salad made with brown rice, but it's equally delicious when made with farro, barley, wild rice, quinoa, or bulgur. A great way to use the bounty from your garden, this salad makes a terrific bed for grilled salmon or chicken.

WHAT YOU'LL NEED

- 3 cups/495 to 690 g freshly cooked grain of your choice (see Cook's Note, page 143)
- ½ cup/120 ml extra-virgin olive oil
- ¼ cup/60 ml red wine vinegar
- Salt and freshly ground black pepper
- 1 cup/155 g cherry or pear tomatoes, halved, or quartered if large
- 4 green onions, white and tender green parts, finely chopped
- 1 medium zucchini, finely diced
- ¼ cup/15 g packed basil leaves, thinly sliced

Put the warm grain in a large serving bowl. In a small bowl, whisk together the olive oil, red wine vinegar, 1 tsp salt, and ½ tsp pepper. Taste for seasoning and add more salt and pepper if needed. Toss the grain with some of the dressing, and reserve the rest for finishing.

When the grain has cooled, add the tomatoes, green onions, zucchini, and basil to the bowl and toss to combine. Add more dressing if needed. Refrigerate the salad and any leftover dressing for up to 12 hours. Remove the salad from the refrigerator 30 minutes before serving and toss with additional dressing, if needed.

BARLEY SALAD WITH PANCETTA, CORN, AND CURRY VINAIGRETTE

—

This simple salad with bits of salty pancetta, sweet corn, and fresh chives, tossed with a slightly sweet curry dressing, is a real crowd-pleaser. Feel free to adjust the vegetables and meat to suit your family's taste. If you have tomatoes from your garden, they make a lovely addition, too. Tossing the dressing with the barley when it is warm helps the barley absorb the flavors rapidly.

WHAT YOU'LL NEED

Curry Dressing

- ⅓ cup/65 g sugar
- ½ cup/120 ml red wine vinegar
- ½ cup/120 ml vegetable oil
- 2 tsp fresh lemon juice
- 1 tsp Worcestershire sauce
- 1 tsp curry powder
- ½ tsp garlic salt
- ½ tsp dry mustard

- 3 cups/690 g freshly cooked barley (see page 29)
- 1 Tbsp extra-virgin olive oil
- One ½-in-/12-mm-thick slice pancetta, finely chopped
- 2 cups/340 g corn kernels, cut fresh from the cob, or frozen kernels, defrosted
- 1 European cucumber, finely diced
- ¼ cup/15 g finely chopped fresh chives, plus whole chives for garnish
- 1 butterhead lettuce, leaves separated

TO MAKE THE CURRY DRESSING: In a mixing bowl, whisk together the sugar, vinegar, vegetable oil, lemon juice, Worcestershire, curry powder, garlic salt, and dry mustard until blended. Set aside or refrigerate for up to 1 week.

While the barley is still warm, transfer it to a large serving bowl and stir in ⅓ cup/75 ml of the dressing. Set aside. In a medium skillet, heat the olive oil over medium-high heat and cook the pancetta until it is crispy. Remove to paper towels to cool and drain. In the same skillet, sauté the corn for 2 to 3 minutes, until it softens. Add the cooled pancetta and the corn to the barley and toss in the cucumber and chopped chives. Drizzle some of the dressing over the top of the salad and toss again, adding more dressing if needed. Serve the salad in lettuce cups, garnished with whole chives.

LEMONY QUINOA SALAD WITH TOMATO AND GREEN ONIONS

This zesty salad studded with juicy vine-ripened tomatoes, green onions, and crunchy celery works as a light luncheon, or it can be a bed for grilled fish or poultry. The lemon vinaigrette is terrific with other grains as well; try barley, rice, or bulgur.

WHAT YOU'LL NEED

- 1½ cups/280 g prewashed quinoa
- 2¼ cups/540 ml chicken or vegetable broth or water
- Salt
- Grated zest of 2 lemons, plus 3 Tbsp fresh lemon juice
- ½ cup/120 ml extra-virgin olive oil
- 1 Tbsp finely chopped shallot

- 1 garlic clove, minced
- Freshly ground black pepper
- 1 cup/155 g finely chopped tomatoes (out of season use cherry or pear tomatoes, quartered)
- 3 celery ribs, finely chopped
- 3 green onions, white and tender green parts, finely chopped

Combine the quinoa, chicken broth, 1 tsp salt, and half the lemon zest in a medium rice cooker. Cover and set to the regular cycle. When the cycle is complete, turn off the machine and allow the quinoa to continue steaming for an additional 5 minutes. Transfer the quinoa to a large bowl and let cool.

In a small bowl, whisk together the olive oil, lemon juice, remaining lemon zest, shallot, and garlic. Season with salt and pepper. Pour half the dressing over the cooled quinoa; reserve the rest for finishing. Fold in the tomatoes, celery, and green onions and gently toss to combine. Refrigerate the salad and any leftover dressing for up to 24 hours. Remove the salad from the refrigerator 1 hour before serving and toss with additional dressing, if necessary.

GARLICKY GREEN BEANS WITH MIXED VEGETABLE QUINOA PILAF

In this recipe, green beans steam above a quinoa pilaf and then are mixed with a citrus gremolata—an Italian garnish with garlic, parsley, and citrus—for a punch of flavor.

WHAT YOU'LL NEED

- ½ lb/225 g green beans, trimmed and cut into 1-in/2.5-cm pieces
- 2 Tbsp extra-virgin olive oil
- ½ cup/80 g finely chopped sweet yellow onion, such as Vidalia
- 1 cup/190 g prewashed quinoa
- 2¼ cups/540 ml chicken or vegetable broth
- 3 garlic cloves, minced
- Grated zest of 1 lemon
- 1 tsp grated orange zest

- ½ cup/30 g finely chopped fresh flat-leaf parsley
- ½ cup/60 g freshly grated Parmigiano-Reggiano cheese
- 1 cup/160 g finely diced zucchini or summer squash
- ½ cup/85 g corn kernels, cut fresh from the cob, or frozen kernels, defrosted
- ½ cup/85 g shelled English peas, or frozen petite peas, defrosted

Arrange the green beans in the steamer basket and set aside. Set a medium rice cooker to the regular cycle or to quick cook if it's a fuzzy-logic machine. Heat the olive oil and sauté the onion for 2 to 3 minutes, or until it begins to soften. Add the quinoa and cook for 1 minute, stirring to coat with the oil mixture. Add the chicken broth slowly. Arrange the steamer basket over the quinoa.

Cover the rice cooker and reset to the regular cycle. While the quinoa and green beans are cooking, combine the garlic, lemon zest, orange zest, parsley, and Parmigiano in a food processor or blender. Process until the mixture forms a paste and set aside. When the cooking cycle is complete, remove the steamer basket and stir the zucchini, corn, and peas into the quinoa. Cover and continue steaming for an additional 5 minutes on the keep-warm setting or with the machine turned off. (Many rice cookers, including all fuzzy-logic machines, do this automatically.) Meanwhile, transfer the green beans to a mixing bowl and toss with the gremolata. Transfer the quinoa to a platter and top with the green beans before serving.

BLACK KALE, WINTER SQUASH, AND BULGUR PILAF

—

This complete one-pot meal is a great balance of bitter, sweet, and savory, with lots of flavor thrown in for good measure. The good-for-you kale and butternut squash are terrific partners, which complement the chewy texture of the bulgur. This dish works well with farro or barley, too. See the basic recipes on pages 26 and 29 for the correct amounts of liquid and grain.

WHAT YOU'LL NEED

- 1 cup/215 g coarse bulgur
- 2 Tbsp extra-virgin olive oil
- 4 garlic cloves, minced
- ½ cup/80 g finely chopped sweet yellow onion, such as Vidalia
- 1 bunch black kale, tough stems removed, and leaves cut into thin ribbons
- 1 cup/225 g finely chopped butternut squash (or your favorite winter squash), peeled and seeded
- Grated zest of 1 orange
- 3 cups/720 ml chicken or vegetable broth
- 2 Tbsp unsalted butter

Place the bulgur in a sieve and rinse under a steady stream of cool water, stirring the grains. When the water runs clear, stop rinsing and shake the sieve to drain off excess water.

Set a medium rice cooker to the regular cycle or to quick cook if it's a fuzzy-logic machine. Heat the olive oil, add the garlic and onion, and sauté for 3 minutes, or until the onion is softened. Add the kale and squash and sauté for another 3 to 4 minutes, until the kale begins to soften. Add the orange zest and bulgur and turn in the pan, to coat them with the oil. Add the chicken broth.

Cover the rice cooker and reset to the regular cycle. At the end of the cooking cycle, fluff the bulgur and stir in the butter. Allow the bulgur to continue steaming for an additional 5 minutes on the keep-warm setting or with the machine turned off before serving.

BABY ARTICHOKE FARRO PILAF

This makes a terrific side dish, but for me it could be a complete dinner. The baby artichokes cook with farro in a lemon-and-thyme-scented broth, resulting in a zingy dish with lots of flavor. If artichokes are not in season, you can use frozen artichoke hearts.

WHAT YOU'LL NEED

- 1 cup/200 g pearled farro
- 2 Tbsp unsalted butter
- 1 Tbsp extra-virgin olive oil
- ½ cup/80 g finely chopped shallots
- 2 garlic cloves, minced
- 4 baby artichokes, trimmed and quartered (see Cook's Note, page 154)
- Grated zest of 2 lemons, plus ½ cup/120 ml fresh lemon juice

- 1 tsp dried thyme
- 1 bay leaf
- ½ cup/120 ml dry white wine, such as Sauvignon Blanc or Pinot Grigio, or dry vermouth
- ⅔ cup/165 ml chicken or vegetable broth
- 2 Tbsp finely chopped fresh flat-leaf parsley

Place the farro in a sieve and rinse under a steady stream of cool water, stirring the grains. When the water runs clear, stop rinsing and shake the sieve to drain off excess water.

Set a medium rice cooker to the regular cycle or to quick cook if it's a fuzzy-logic machine. Melt the butter with the olive oil, add the shallots and garlic, and sauté for 2 minutes, or until the shallots begin to soften. Add the artichokes, lemon zest, thyme, and bay leaf. Sauté the artichokes for 3 to 4 minutes, turning frequently to coat with the butter mixture. Add the farro and toast the farro for 2 minutes. Slowly pour in the lemon juice, white wine, and chicken broth.

Cover the rice cooker and reset to the regular cycle. When the pilaf is done, check to make sure the artichoke hearts are tender. If they aren't quite done, re-cover and continue steaming for 5 to 10 minutes on the keep-warm setting or with the cooker turned off. (Many rice cookers, including all fuzzy-logic machines, do this automatically.) Remove the bay leaf, transfer the pilaf to a large bowl, and garnish with the parsley before serving.

continued

COOK'S NOTE: *To trim baby artichokes, cut off the stem about ¾ in/2 cm from the top. Then carefully trim away the tough outer leaves, until you reach the tender green leaves. Quarter the artichokes, put them in a bowl, and cover with water. Gently stir in the juice of a lemon to prevent discoloration and set aside until you're ready to use.*

If you're substituting frozen artichoke hearts for the fresh, defrost them and add to the pilaf 5 minutes before the end of the cooking time.

BULGUR RISOTTO WITH MIXED MUSHROOMS

This hearty risotto relies on meaty mushrooms for flavor. Along with the bulgur, the mushrooms also give the risotto a chewy texture. Feel free to substitute your favorite mushrooms. If you use portobellos (which are overgrown cremini), you will need to clean the gills; otherwise the risotto will turn dark. If you can find mushroom broth, use it; it makes a dynamite risotto.

WHAT YOU'LL NEED

- 1 cup/215 g coarse bulgur
- 4 Tbsp/55 g unsalted butter
- 1 Tbsp extra-virgin olive oil
- 2 garlic cloves, minced
- 1 small onion, finely chopped
- ¾ lb/340 g mixed mushrooms, such as cremini, shiitake (stems removed), chanterelle, and oyster, coarsely chopped
- ½ cup/120 ml dry white wine, such as Sauvignon Blanc or Pinot Grigio, or dry vermouth
- 3 cups/720 ml chicken or vegetable broth or, better still, mushroom broth
- ¼ cup/30 g freshly grated Parmigiano-Reggiano cheese
- 2 Tbsp finely chopped fresh flat-leaf parsley

Place the bulgur in a sieve and rinse under a steady stream of cool water, stirring the grains. When the water runs clear, stop rinsing and shake the sieve to drain off excess water.

Set a medium rice cooker to the regular cycle or to quick cook if it's a fuzzy-logic machine. Melt 2 Tbsp of the butter with the olive oil, add the garlic and onion, and sauté for 2 minutes. Add the mushrooms and cook for 4 to 5 minutes, until they begin to color and their liquid begins to evaporate. Add the bulgur and cook for 2 minutes. Gradually add the wine and chicken broth.

Cover the rice cooker and reset to the regular cycle. Set a timer for 20 minutes. When the timer goes off, check to make sure the bulgur is tender. If not, cover and continue steaming for an additional 5 minutes on the keep-warm setting or with the machine turned off. (Many rice cookers, including all fuzzy-logic machines, do this automatically.) Stir in the remaining 2 Tbsp butter, the Parmigiano, and parsley and serve.

SPRING VEGETABLE RISOTTO

This risotto is dotted with beautiful green spring vegetables and makes a lovely vegetarian lunch or dinner. Delicious with a roasted beet and arugula salad, it's simple to make. There is no arduous stirring; the rice cooker takes care of everything.

WHAT YOU'LL NEED

- 1 cup/215 g medium-grain rice, such as Arborio, Carnaroli, or Vialone
- 4 Tbsp/55 g unsalted butter
- 1 garlic clove, minced
- 1 leek, tender white part only, finely chopped
- 1 cup/140 g packed baby spinach, finely chopped
- 1 fennel bulb, wispy ends removed and finely chopped

- ½ cup/120 ml dry white wine, such as Sauvignon Blanc or Pinot Grigio, or dry vermouth
- 2½ cups/600 ml chicken broth
- 1 cup/170 g shelled fresh fava beans (see Cook's Note, page 158)
- 1 cup/170 g shelled English peas
- ⅓ cup/45 g freshly grated Parmigiano-Reggiano cheese
- Salt and freshly ground black pepper

Place the rice in a sieve and rinse under a steady stream of cool water, stirring the grains. When the water runs clear, stop rinsing and shake the sieve to drain off excess water.

Coat the inside of a medium rice cooker with nonstick cooking spray. Set the rice cooker to the regular cycle or to quick cook if it's a fuzzy-logic machine. Melt 2 Tbsp of the butter; add the garlic, leek, spinach, and fennel; and sauté for 2 to 3 minutes, or until the leek is softened. Add the wine and bring to a boil. Add the rice and chicken broth and stir to distribute the ingredients.

Cover the rice cooker and reset to the regular cycle. Set a timer for 15 minutes. When the timer goes off, stir in the fava beans and peas. Cover and allow to steam for an additional 5 minutes on the keep-warm setting or with the machine turned off. (Many rice cookers, including all fuzzy-logic machines, do this automatically.) Stir in the remaining 2 Tbsp butter and the Parmigiano. Season with salt and pepper. Serve immediately.

continued

COOK'S NOTE: *To remove the tougher skin from fava beans, blanch them in boiling water for 1 minute, drain in a colander, and when cooled, slip off the skins.*

Many times in restaurants, you will get a risotto that isn't creamy; it happens when the cook is distracted and doesn't watch the rice. Well-made risotto has some thickened liquid along with the rice; that's what makes it creamy, rather than a gelatinous mass. As the rice sits on your plate, it is still cooking and will absorb the remaining liquid.

SUMMER SQUASH RISOTTO

This is a terrific recipe to serve when the squashes in your garden are threatening to overtake your home. Perfumed with fresh mint and enriched with butter and Parmesan cheese, this dish will have your family asking for it again and again. I like to use a combination of yellow squash and zucchini for the variations in texture and color.

WHAT YOU'LL NEED

- 1 cup/215 g medium-grain rice, such as Arborio or Carnaroli
- 4 Tbsp/55 g unsalted butter
- 1 Tbsp extra-virgin olive oil
- ½ cup/80 g finely chopped sweet yellow onion, such as Vidalia
- 3 cups/720 ml chicken or vegetable broth
- 2 medium zucchini, finely diced
- 1 medium yellow squash, finely diced
- 2 Tbsp finely chopped fresh mint
- ¼ cup/30 g freshly grated Parmigiano-Reggiano cheese

Place the rice in a sieve and rinse under a steady stream of cool water, stirring the grains. When the water runs clear, stop rinsing and shake the sieve to drain off excess water.

Set a medium rice cooker to the regular cycle or to quick cook if it's a fuzzy-logic machine. Melt 2 Tbsp of the butter with the olive oil, add the onion, and sauté for 2 to 3 minutes, or until the onion is softened. Add the rice and toast for 2 to 3 minutes, stirring. Gradually add the chicken broth.

Cover the rice cooker and set to the regular cycle. Set a timer for 15 minutes. When the timer goes off, add the zucchini and yellow squash. Cover and cook for an additional 5 minutes and then check to make sure the rice is al dente (still firm to the bite). Stir in the mint and remaining 2 Tbsp butter. Serve the risotto in shallow bowls, garnished with Parmigiano.

VEGETABLE BIRYANI

This delicious vegetable biryani has sweet notes from the peas, carrots, and sweet potatoes; spicy notes from the Madras curry powder, ginger, and garlic; and a lovely fragrance from the basmati rice. If you're looking for a shortcut, you can substitute 1 Tbsp biryani paste for the ginger, garlic, and curry powder.

WHAT YOU'LL NEED

- 1 cup/215 g basmati rice
- 2 Tbsp vegetable oil
- 2 garlic cloves, minced
- 1 tsp grated peeled fresh ginger
- 2 tsp Madras curry powder
- 1 medium red onion, finely chopped
- 1 cup/225 g sweet potato, peeled and finely chopped
- ½ lb/225 g green beans, trimmed and cut into 1-in/2.5-cm lengths
- 2 medium carrots, peeled and finely chopped

- 2 cups/480 ml chicken or vegetable broth
- 1 cup/160 g cauliflower florets, cut into 1-in/2.5-cm pieces
- 1 cup/170 g shelled English peas, or frozen petite peas, defrosted
- ¼ cup/15 g finely chopped fresh cilantro
- Raita (page 163) for serving
- Assorted chutneys and lime pickles for serving

Place the rice in a sieve and rinse under a steady stream of cool water, stirring the grains. When the water runs clear, stop rinsing and shake the sieve to drain off excess water.

Set a medium rice cooker to the regular cycle or to quick cook if it's a fuzzy-logic machine. Heat the vegetable oil; add the garlic, ginger, and curry powder; and sauté for 30 seconds, or until fragrant. Add the onion and sweet potato and stir to coat with the curry mixture. Add the green beans, carrots, and rice and stir to combine. Gradually add the chicken broth and cauliflower, stirring to combine.

Cover and reset the rice cooker to the regular cycle. At the end of the cooking cycle, stir in the peas. Allow the biryani to continue steaming for an additional 5 minutes on the keep-warm setting or with the machine turned off. (Many rice cookers, including all fuzzy-logic machines, do this automatically.) Remove from the rice cooker, transfer to a platter, and garnish with the cilantro. Serve the biryani with the raita and assorted chutneys and lime pickles.

CURRIED CAULIFLOWER, PURPLE POTATOES, AND BASMATI RICE WITH RAITA

The curry and rice cook upside down, but they work beautifully together: While the curry bubbles underneath, the basmati rice steams to perfection in the steamer basket. The vegetables here are traditional—cauliflower, peas, and potatoes—but you can substitute your favorites. Just make sure the more tender vegetables are added at the end of the cooking time, so they don't disintegrate. I've chosen to use purple potatoes for color and flavor here, but you can substitute any low-starch potato, such as red, Yukon gold, or white creamers. The raita makes a great accompaniment for the curry, as do chutneys and lime pickle or your favorite condiments for Indian food.

WHAT YOU'LL NEED

- 1 cup/215 g basmati rice
- 2 Tbsp extra-virgin olive oil
- 1 medium red onion, finely chopped
- 2 garlic cloves, minced
- 1 tsp grated peeled fresh ginger
- 2 tsp Madras curry powder
- 2 medium carrots, peeled and coarsely chopped
- 2 cups/320 g cauliflower florets

- ½ lb/225 g small purple potatoes, halved or quartered
- One 14½-oz/415-g can coconut milk
- 1½ cups/360 ml chicken or vegetable broth
- 1 cup/170 g shelled English peas, or frozen petite peas, defrosted
- Raita (recipe follows) for serving
- Assorted chutneys and lime pickles for serving

Place the rice in a sieve and rinse under a steady stream of cool water, stirring the grains. When the water runs clear, stop rinsing and shake the sieve to drain off excess water.

Set a medium rice cooker to the regular cycle or to quick cook if it's a fuzzy-logic machine. Heat the olive oil; add the onion, garlic, ginger, and curry powder; and sauté for 2 minutes, or until fragrant. Add the carrots, cauliflower, and potatoes and turn to coat with the curry powder. Gradually add the coconut milk and chicken broth and stir to combine. Fit the steamer basket with a coffee filter or a sheet of paper towel, and place the rice on top. Place the steamer basket in the rice cooker.

Cover the rice cooker and reset to the regular cycle. Set a timer for 20 minutes. When the timer goes off, check to make sure the potatoes are tender; the tip of a sharp paring knife should go through easily. Make sure the rice is tender, too. Stir in the peas, cover, and continue steaming for an additional 5 minutes on the keep-warm setting or with the machine turned off. (Many rice cookers, including fuzzy-logic machines, do this automatically.) Transfer the rice to a serving platter, and spoon the curry over the rice. Serve the curry with the raita and assorted chutneys and lime pickles.

RAITA

MAKES 2 CUPS/480 ML

There are probably as many variations of raita—a cooling, yogurt-based sauce—as there are cooks in India and Pakistan. This one features cucumber and mint, which go well with the curried veggies.

WHAT YOU'LL NEED

- 1 European cucumber, peeled and grated
- 1 cup/240 ml plain yogurt
- 1 garlic clove, minced

- 2 Tbsp chopped fresh mint
- ½ tsp salt
- 3 or 4 dashes hot sauce (optional)

Place the cucumber in a sieve or colander and allow to drain for 30 minutes. Squeeze dry and transfer to a mixing bowl. Add the yogurt, garlic, mint, and salt. Taste for seasoning and add a few dashes of hot sauce, if desired. Store, covered, in the refrigerator for up to 4 days. Stir before serving to blend.

KITCHEN SINK
NOT-FRIED RICE
—

Fried rice is usually made with cold cooked rice, but this one is made with freshly cooked rice and whatever vegetables you have on hand. The recommended amounts of liquid, vegetables, and sauce are your guides. After that, you can make this your own. If I have them on hand, I like to include bits of leftover cooked meats, seafood, or poultry when sautéing the vegetables.

WHAT YOU'LL NEED

- 2 cups/430 g long-grain rice
- 2 Tbsp vegetable oil
- 2 garlic cloves, minced
- 1 tsp grated peeled fresh ginger
- 1 medium carrot, peeled and coarsely grated
- 1 celery rib, finely chopped
- ½ cup/85 g corn kernels cut from the cob, or frozen kernels, defrosted
- ¼ cup/60 ml tamari or soy sauce
- ¼ cup/60 ml rice wine

- 2½ cups/600 ml chicken or vegetable broth
- 2 large eggs, lightly beaten
- 1 head baby bok choy, root end trimmed, leaves finely chopped
- ½ cup/70 g bean sprouts (see Cook's Note)
- 2 green onions, white and tender green parts, finely chopped
- 1 to 2 tsp toasted sesame oil

Place the rice in a sieve and rinse under a steady stream of cool water, stirring the grains. When the water runs clear, stop rinsing and shake the sieve to drain off excess water.

Set a medium rice cooker to the regular cycle or to quick cook if it's a fuzzy-logic machine. Heat 1 Tbsp of the vegetable oil; add the garlic, ginger, carrot, and celery; and sauté for 2 to 3 minutes, or until the vegetables are softened. Add the corn and rice and toast in the oil for 2 minutes, tossing frequently. Gradually add the tamari, rice wine, and chicken broth.

Cover the rice cooker and reset to the regular cycle. While the rice is cooking, heat the remaining 1 Tbsp oil in a small skillet over medium heat. Add the eggs and cook until set on the bottom. Flip them and cook until set on the second side. Remove from the skillet to a cutting board and cut the omelet into thin strips.

When the cooking cycle is complete, add the bok choy and eggs to the rice, stirring to combine. Cover and continue steaming for an additional 3 minutes on the keep-warm setting or with the machine turned off. (Many rice cookers, including all fuzzy-logic machines, do this automatically.) Transfer the rice to a serving bowl or platter. Garnish with the bean sprouts and chopped green onions, drizzle with a bit of toasted sesame oil, and serve.

———

COOK'S NOTE: *Broccoli or radish sprouts can be substituted for the bean sprouts to give the rice another delicious note.*

BEER-STEAMED RICE WITH BLACK BEANS, CORN, AND TOMATOES

Colorful, spicy, and simple to assemble, this dish is terrific to serve anytime. It's delicious as a main course, garnished with sliced avocado, queso fresco, *and sour cream, or as a bed for grilled meats, poultry, or seafood. Try this using brown basmati or long-grain white rice.*

WHAT YOU'LL NEED

- 2 cups/430 g brown basmati or long-grain white rice
- 2 Tbsp vegetable oil
- 2 garlic cloves, minced
- ½ cup/80 g chopped red onion
- 1 cup/155 g cherry or pear tomatoes, quartered, or grape tomatoes, halved
- ½ cup/80 g chopped green bell pepper
- 1 jalapeño chile, seeded, deribbed, and finely chopped
- ½ tsp ground cumin
- ½ tsp dried oregano

- 3 cups/720 ml pale Mexican beer or vegetable broth
- One 14½-oz/415-g can black beans, rinsed and drained
- 1½ cups/255 g corn kernels, cut fresh from the cob, or frozen kernels, defrosted
- 1 Hass avocado, pitted, peeled, and sliced
- 1 cup/225 g crumbled *queso fresco*
- 1 cup/240 ml sour cream
- ¼ cup/15 g chopped fresh cilantro

Place the rice in a sieve and rinse under a steady stream of cool water, stirring the grains. When the water runs clear, stop rinsing and shake the sieve to drain off excess water.

Set a medium rice cooker to the regular cycle or to quick cook if it's a fuzzy-logic machine. Heat the vegetable oil, add the garlic and onion, and sauté for 2 minutes. Add the tomatoes, bell pepper, jalapeño, cumin, and oregano and sauté for another 2 minutes, or until the vegetables begin to soften. Add the rice and stir to coat with the sauce. Add the beer.

Cover the rice cooker and reset to the regular cycle. At the end of the cooking cycle, stir the rice and add the black beans and corn. Cover and continue steaming for an additional 5 minutes on the keep-warm setting or with the machine turned off. (Many rice cookers, including all fuzzy-logic machines, do this automatically.) Serve, garnished with avocado, *queso fresco*, sour cream, and cilantro.

RED BEANS AND RICE

Mondays in New Orleans were traditionally wash days, and the woman of the house would put on a pot of spicy red beans flavored with a ham hock or andouille sausage. The pot would simmer all day long until the family was ready to enjoy the beans over steamed rice. This one-pot version of the original is filled with sausage, red beans, spices, and rice. You just need to flip the switch, and dinner will be ready!

WHAT YOU'LL NEED

- ½ cup/110 g long-grain rice
- 2 Tbsp extra-virgin olive oil
- ½ lb/225 g smoked sausage, cut into small dice
- ½ cup/80 g finely chopped sweet yellow onion, such as Vidalia
- 2 garlic cloves, minced
- ½ cup/80 g finely chopped celery
- ½ cup/80 g finely chopped green bell pepper

- 2 tsp dried thyme
- Pinch of cayenne pepper
- 1 bay leaf
- One 14½-oz/415-g can red beans, rinsed and drained
- 3 cups/720 ml chicken or vegetable broth
- Salt and freshly ground black pepper
- Assorted hot sauces for serving

Place the rice in a sieve and rinse under a steady stream of cool water, stirring the grains. When the water runs clear, stop rinsing and shake the sieve to drain off excess water.

Set a medium rice cooker to the regular cycle or to quick cook if it's a fuzzy-logic machine. Heat the olive oil; add the sausage, onion, garlic, celery, bell pepper, thyme, cayenne, and bay leaf; and sauté for 2 to 3 minutes, or until the vegetables are softened. Add the red beans, rice, and chicken broth.

Cover the rice cooker and reset to the regular cycle. Set a timer for 30 minutes. When the timer goes off, check to make sure the rice is tender. Season the red beans with salt and pepper, if needed, and serve with assorted hot sauces.

BROCCOLI RABE AND PANCETTA BREAD PUDDING

—

This savory bread pudding studded with nuggets of pancetta and garlicky broccoli rabe makes a terrific side dish to serve with grilled meats, poultry, and seafood. Feel free to substitute your favorite bitter green for the broccoli rabe.

WHAT YOU'LL NEED

- 2 Tbsp extra-virgin olive oil
- One ½-in-/12-mm-thick slice pancetta, finely diced
- 2 garlic cloves, minced
- ¼ cup/40 g finely chopped onion
- 1 head broccoli rabe, tough stems removed, finely chopped
- 1½ tsp salt
- ½ tsp freshly ground black pepper
- 4 cups/460 g torn Italian or French bread with a soft crust
- 4 large eggs
- 1 cup/240 ml heavy cream

Coat the inside of a medium rice cooker with nonstick cooking spray. Set the rice cooker to the regular cycle or to quick cook if it's a fuzzy-logic machine. Heat the olive oil, add the pancetta, and cook until it becomes crispy. Add the garlic and cook for 1 minute. Add the onion, broccoli rabe, salt, and pepper and sauté for 5 to 6 minutes, until the broccoli rabe is softened.

Put the bread into a large mixing bowl. In another bowl, beat the eggs and cream together. Pour the mixture over the bread and stir to combine. Pour the bread-egg mixture into the rice cooker and stir so that the bits of vegetable and pancetta are distributed throughout the mixture.

Cover the rice cooker and reset to the regular cycle. At the end of the cooking cycle, uncover and allow to rest for 15 minutes on the keep-warm setting or with the machine turned off. Serve warm.

ASPARAGUS AND GOAT CHEESE FRITTATA

When I put these ingredients in my rice cooker, I knew the flavors would complement each other, but I wondered what the dish would look like. It was lovely! The soft, melting goat cheese mingled with the asparagus and creamy eggs. The frittata makes a great light supper or luncheon dish; serve it with a fruit salad.

WHAT YOU'LL NEED

- 1 Tbsp olive oil
- 1 Tbsp finely chopped spring onion or green onion, white part only
- ½ lb/225 g asparagus, trimmed and cut into ½-in/12-mm pieces
- 4 large eggs
- ⅓ cup/75 ml heavy cream
- 1 tsp salt
- ¼ tsp Tabasco sauce
- ½ cup/30 g crumbled goat cheese

Set a medium rice cooker to the regular cycle or to quick cook if it's a fuzzy-logic machine. Heat the olive oil and sauté the spring onion for 1 minute. Add the asparagus and cook for another 3 minutes, or until the asparagus begins to soften. In a medium mixing bowl, whisk together the eggs, cream, salt, and Tabasco. Pour the egg mixture over the asparagus and sprinkle with the goat cheese.

Cover the rice cooker and reset to the regular cycle. The frittata will take 3 to 4 minutes to cook. Allow it to continue steaming, covered, for an additional 6 minutes on the keep-warm setting or with the machine turned off. (Many rice cookers, including all fuzzy-logic machines, do this automatically.) Serve warm or at room temperature.

INDEX

ACKNOWLEDGMENTS

I find myself grateful for so many things in life. When it comes to this book, there are several people without whom it would not have been possible. First to Bill LeBlond, until recently at Chronicle, who was my advocate for this book. I'm so grateful for all that Bill has done for me while he was there and feel blessed to have worked with him even for a short while. *Grazie*, Bill, for having faith in me, and in this project; I just hope it didn't push you into retirement!

I've dedicated this book to my agent, Susan Ginsburg Webman, and her husband, Jerry, who went the distance, taking time out from their Italian vacation to come visit me in a small Umbrian hill town for the afternoon. I'm grateful to Susan for her guidance and her friendship and for so many other things that would not fit on this page. Suffice it to say she's an all-star!

My home team—my husband, Chuck, and our children—have been a tremendous support, sending me to Italy to live and learn Italian and eating all the test recipes. I'm grateful beyond measure to have such a supportive family and extended family. In Italy, I could not have written this book without the support of *la famiglia* Angelini and their staff at Enoteca Properzio, in Spello. I was given a table to work at in their gorgeous garden, sipping a few glasses of world-class wine along the way and eating mouthwatering foods. Thanks to Roberto, Daniela, Irene, Luca, Carlo, Camelia, Tanya, Kaoma, and Chiara for making me feel at home.

At Chronicle, I'd like to thank my editor, Amy Treadwell, for her hard work on my behalf, and Dawn Yanagihara, for taking over midstream and shepherding the book through production. I must be living right to have Deborah Kops, copy editor extraordinaire, working with me again to shape and clarify this book. Thank you, Deborah, for your gift of making things clear and coherent, from the instructions to the recipe lists; I'm grateful. Thanks also to Peter Perez, David Hawk, Alice Chau, Beth Steiner, and Doug Ogan.

Industry professionals were generous with their knowledge and machines, and I'd like to especially thank Sara de la Hera, of Fagor, and Krista Erickson, at Zojirushi, for their support. No cookbook author can write a book on her own. We are inspired by others who have led the way, and I'm especially grateful to Rick Rodgers and Lora Brody for their encouragement and their friendship; I could not have asked for better mentors and friends.

My students and the cooking schools where I teach are an inspiration to me; they survive and thrive in the age of Amazon, Walmart, and Costco. Thanks to all the cooking schools that have invited me into their kitchens over the years to allow me to share my passion and to meet the students who buy my books and cook from them. Here in San Diego I'm indebted to the Harrington brothers, Kellie Palermo, and the awesome staff at Specialty Produce, who provide me with organic, sustainable produce each week, and challenge me as I write the weekly recipes for their Farmer's Market Box.